"The world feels increasingly complex and filled with uncertainty, volatility, and ambiguity. A new type of adaptive, faithful leader is needed. Through great storytelling and practical examples, Sam Van Eman's *Disruptive Discipleship* shows us how we might welcome—and even pursue—the disruptions of life as a means to growing deeper in our faith, hope, and love."

Chris Cooke, executive director, PULSE

"At a time when so many of us are increasingly wandering in search of comfort, we secretly prefer to be stuck instead of doing the necessary hard work before us. With courageous wit and deeply personal insights, Sam Van Eman and his *Disruptive Discipleship* guided me through how to honestly identify my current path and forge a better way to lasting spiritual growth."

Ryan Keith, president, Forgotten Voices

"Everybody gets stuck or stalled in their walk with Christ. Not everybody has a clear idea of how to move beyond that place. Van Eman draws his reader into the kind of self-reflection that can assist in crafting a personalized experience of disruption designed to create movement. For the mentor and for the disciple of Christ looking 'to grow in faith on purpose,' this book provides a fresh approach to becoming more like Christ. *Disruptive Discipleship* stays away from prepackaged solutions and experiences and instead leans into process over productivity, but without getting stalled by inactivity. Van Eman goes beyond coaching the reader in merely designing experiences by helping us know how to practically engage with our disruptions to really make the growth we've gained stick."

Jana Sundene, associate professor, Trinity International University, coauthor of *Shaping the Journey of Emerging Adults*

"In a culture where the extremes of chasing the next high or staying in our comfort zone tend to pervade, Sam Van Eman offers a brilliant alternative: purposeful risk-taking tha ... ked with wisdom, wit, and personal ... risk that leads to real faith. Sam invit ... n't leave us there. His honest and ho ... e feeling stuck, lost, or simply want t ... nture of *Disruptive Discipleship* awaits.

Erica Young Reitz, director, Senior EXIT, CCO, author of *After College*

"I've always viewed disruptions as the annoying experiences that rearrange my schedule and mess with my plans. Until now. Sam Van Eman disrupted my way of thinking, jolting me to see how disruptions actually move us toward spiritual maturity. With his trademark storytelling and wisdom, Sam leads us all down a path of purposeful growth. This hope-filled book helps us figure out where we're stuck, then offers practical approaches to move us into new seasons of growth."

Jennifer Dukes Lee, author of *The Happiness Dare* and *Love Idol*

"*Disruptive Discipleship* explores how to get unstuck and say yes to the good reality we were created for. We don't learn or grow just by getting new information. We have to risk experimenting with new practices, experiences, and challenges. Sam Van Eman is an enthusiastic, honest, and seasoned guide to this adventure."

Mark Scandrette, author of *Free, Practicing the Way of Jesus,* and *Belonging and Becoming*

DISRUPTIVE DISCIPLESHIP

The Power of Breaking Routine
to Kickstart Your Faith

Sam Van Eman

IVP Books

An imprint of InterVarsity Press
Downers Grove, Illinois

InterVarsity Press
P.O. Box 1400, Downers Grove, IL 60515-1426
ivpress.com
email@ivpress.com

InterVarsity Press® is the book-publishing division of InterVarsity Christian Fellowship/USA, a movement of students and faculty active on campus at hundreds of universities, colleges, and schools of nursing in the United States of America, and a member movement of the International Fellowship of Evangelical Students. For information about local and regional activities, visit intervarsity.org.

All Scripture quotations, unless otherwise indicated, are taken from The Holy Bible, New International Version®, NIV®. Copyright © 1973, 1978, 1984, 2011 by Biblica, Inc.™ Used by permission of Zondervan. All rights reserved worldwide. www.zondervan.com The "NIV" and "New International Version" are trademarks registered in the United States Patent and Trademark Office by Biblica, Inc.™

While any stories in this book are true, some names and identifying information may have been changed to protect the privacy of individuals.

Cover design: Cindy Kiple
Interior design: Jeanna Wiggins
Images: styled waves: © CSA-Archive/iStockphoto
*   ship illustrations: © lokichen/iStockphoto*

ISBN 978-0-8308-4508-8 (print)
ISBN 978-0-8308-9081-1 (digital)

Printed in the United States of America ∞

Library of Congress Cataloging-in-Publication Data
A catalog record for this book is available from the Library of Congress.

P 22 21 20 19 18 17 16 15 14 13 12 11 10 9 8 7 6 5 4 3 2 1

Y 34 33 32 31 30 29 28 27 26 25 24 23 22 21 20 19 18 17

To Paul Harbison,

who disrupts for the sake of shalom.

To all who have suffered (a little or a lot) with me on purpose.

I'm ready to go again when you are.

"Let perseverance finish its work so that you may be

mature and complete, not lacking anything."

James 1:4

CONTENTS

AUTHOR NOTE

Scott pulled a few of us together at the diner and said cautiously, "I don't know what I'm looking for, but I'm in a slump. I just feel sort of bleh. Is there anything we could do about it together?"

Moments like these indicate the need for change, which, for the one needing the change, can be revealing (and maybe even embarrassing).

What Scott did took humility and courage, a rather potent combination. At the back of this book, you'll find questions that others can ask you when you do what Scott did. In time, you may need to ask those same questions of others. We grow best when we grow together.

Portions of three stories you'll read, including the caving story, my encounter with Juancito, and the discussion of Jesus' rebuke of Peter, were originally shared with the community at TheHigh Calling.org, now hosted by TheologyofWork.org. While all stories in *Disruptive Discipleship* are real, some names and identifying details have been altered to protect the privacy of individuals.

INTRODUCTION

We Can't Not Change

My scooter sat in the cold garage all winter. Come spring, when I needed to run an errand across town, it wouldn't start. The battery was drained too low for the auto-ignition to work. My mind was running through solutions for the scooter as well as alternatives for the errand, when a light dawned. I reached down, exposed the kick-start post, gave it a swift pump with my foot, then another, and the engine fired up. The battery recharged, and the auto-ignition resumed fulfilling its purpose.

One of the best ways to deal with a half-dead battery—whether actual or metaphorical in our lives as Christians—is to step back and consider a new approach. Alternatives are rarely obvious. They're also often inconvenient—and even painful under certain circumstances. But they're necessary if we want to go somewhere.

In a broad sense, that's what this book is about: finding ways to go somewhere when your routine methods seem to be keeping you stuck. I could have complained about the scooter or kicked *it* instead of the foot post out of frustration. I could have blamed the guy who sold it to me for not explaining how to winterize the battery, or my wife for suggesting I dig the thing out of the shed to run my errand in the first place. I might have done all of these had I not remembered there was a kick-start.

Immaturity results in a host of issues: high blood pressure, anger, tiffs with neighbors and family members, and even a few sore toes. We don't have to be *Anger Management* material to qualify as immature. We only need to respond poorly to whatever situation we face, like the protagonist in the Brothers Grimm tale "The Ungrateful Son," whose meal turned into a curse after he hid it from his father. As the story goes, "The son wanted to put the roasted chicken back onto the table, but when he reached for it, it had turned into a large toad, which jumped into his face and sat there and never went away again."[1]

Yikes. I'd like to say we're fortunate to escape such immediate and noticeable consequences, but I'm not sure *fortunate* is the right word. The consequences to my immaturity are often so subtle, so gradual, that I miss the lesson to be learned, or I don't even see there *is* a problem. At least for the son in this story, the toad proved the seriousness of an ongoing, unaddressed conflict in his family. Clarity like that highlights the impact of our actions in a real way, forcing us to face the truth that may be, literally, right in front of us. Unfortunately, it typically doesn't happen this way. We miss the lesson, and the result is similar to the outcome for the son: "And thus he went to and fro in the world without rest."

How long can an employee believe skirting around the truth will produce a good career? How long can a girlfriend believe her abusive boyfriend will grow kinder? How long can a church leader believe he can balance ministry with his penchant for illicit materials and behaviors? How long can a college student believe playing Nintendo's *R.B.I. Baseball* with his hallmates won't affect his grades? (Not long, said my mid-semester failure notice. Not long.) Roof leaks don't repair themselves, and hearts don't grow healthy from planning to exercise. It's like returning my scooter to the garage and thinking the dead battery would somehow work the next time.

If this book is broadly about going somewhere when we feel stuck, it's more specifically about growing up when we've been acting like children. How might this happen outside of persistent prayer or life's unwelcomed challenges that *force* growth upon us? One way is by adding intentional, out-of-the-ordinary disruptions to our daily routine. Disrupting *every* day's routine would lead to chaos, but an occasional shift in the schedule can offer a world of good.

In the Coalition for Christian Outreach (CCO), we refer to these intentional disruptions as "designed experiences." In fact, I work in a department called Experiential Designs—XD for short—which has a forty-year history of delivering customized learning moments for groups, such as six-week mountaineering trips for college students and interactive retreats for board members. We don't create this stuff from scratch—not all of it, at least; we adapt work others pioneered before us and alongside us.

We believe Jesus can use any shift to transform his people. So designed experiences include signing up for a marathon, donating all but a week's worth of clothing (and committing not to replace what you gave away), agreeing to mentor a young professional or newly married couple, or unplugging a favorite streaming service. The list is endless, really. As long as it causes a bit of anxiety in anticipation of being shooed from the nest, we see results.

The first summer that my wife and I were on staff at a summer camp, we served as the outdoor adventure coordinators. Our job was to take cabin counselors and campers hiking, biking, caving, and rock climbing. The initial camps went fine, but something felt empty about our approach, despite everyone having a good time. So Julie and I gathered advice from veterans and took a new approach. This involved converting activities from thrill-seeker entertainment into catalysts for connections, from independent focal points to integrated waypoints. In this manner, we altered the relationship campers had with each activity. For example, instead of treating caving like the icing on a cake, we turned it into the baking soda.

The results amazed us. At the close of our first redesigned week, we gathered with the high school campers and asked for feedback. One by one, they shared how God had spoken to them in fresh ways, how they felt compelled to trust more and fear less, and how the tiny messages we had built activities around became the highlights of their time at camp.

"Wait a minute," I said, interrupting the group. "What about the caving trip and our day on the rock face? As staff, we thought those went pretty well. Maybe not?"

"Oh, no," a girl said. "Caving was totally awesome!"

A boy jumped in after her. "Yeah, this was my seventh year at camp. I've gone to that cave every year, but this was definitely the best."

Others added similar comments, yet not one listed caving itself as the highlight—only what they gained from it. We prodded further, and they explained that something about connecting what we did with why we did it turned the activities into meaningful experiences. From climbing, they grew in faith. From whitewater rafting, they grew to love each other as a team (especially after good rowing and communication saved a camper named Kenny from nearly drowning). Each evaluation clarified my understanding of what can happen when we break routine for the right reasons and in the right ways: we grow in faith, hope, and love.

We can't afford to stay at our current maturity level any more than a baby can stay a baby. The teenagers who wrote, "Don't ever change!" in my high school yearbook couldn't stay the same. Young professionals can't; middle-aged mothers and fathers and accountants can't. The cost of staying put is simply too great. Disciples are students and followers of Jesus, which means we study his ways and then grow in them. We don't have to wait for life to bring us opportunities to mature. We can exercise our God-given ability to take initiative to pursue growth in faith, hope, and love, particularly in experiences that put these three to the test. That's what *Disruptive Discipleship* is about.

GROWTH ON PURPOSE

In James 1:4, the apostle wrote, "Let perseverance finish its work so that you may be mature and complete, not lacking anything." This verse came to mind as I watched a healthcare commercial that showed a man buried in a recliner with junk food. One day, he got up and began removing the fabric, then the padding, and finally the outer frame and hardware. He was left with a simple wooden kitchen chair, which he sat on and found uncomfortable. Then he decided to go for a jog. I thought, *That's the idea behind purposeful growth.*

Mature people make good decisions about their physical lives. They also make good decisions about mental health, relationships, and spirituality. They stay calm; they know how to delay pleasure; they foster trust in their communities. Simply put, they lead healthier, fuller, more peaceful lives. And they do it because they have greater amounts of faith, hope, and love.

When I act like a child (and I do often enough), I throw tantrums to get what I can't imagine waiting for. In those moments, I need the good Parent, who lets me cry it out. This is how God introduces us to the first stages of faith: "Provision will come," he communicates, "just not now and not necessarily in the way you're demanding it." Here we learn patience as we persevere through small trials that become big trials. So James offered a picture of a time when our maturity will be so robust that, despite apparent lack, it will be as if we are "not lacking anything."

I've been referring to voluntary experiences, like summer camp. However, a lot of maturity comes from unplanned experiences—

betrayals, health diagnoses, promotions (trials aren't always negative). Life runs comfortably until this or that bit of news jolts us. Sometimes we crash. Most times we find a way to fly. And then we rest on a branch with a fresh view, stronger resolve, and fewer fears about the next trial. We mature, lacking less than we used to.

Enjoy that fresh view. It's good to have a season of rest and even plenty. But Jesus wants us to take the hard and narrow way, where we learn that lack is more of a mindset than a reality. We can choose to linger in comfort and independence, or we can choose to toughen up.

When I landed my first post-college job, I created a budget before getting paid. I knew the discipline would be good for me. I also knew I would have to cut coupons and take care of my old car. I was earning enough to rent a bigger apartment and purchase a new vehicle, but I chose to install voluntary limits. Having been raised by a father and grandfather who lost the family estate through decades of bad moves, I chose to exercise lack on purpose. This seemingly inconsequential decision bore significant dividends, particularly in the areas of faith and love.

Whether planning an overnight hike or nixing chocolate for Lent, designed experiences help us uncover what curbs and what catalyzes our growth as followers of Christ. If we want our road rage to decrease and our compassion to increase, worry to be replaced by serenity, financial fear to meet generosity, and if we have any desire to learn to wait, forgo, remain calm, listen, forgive, press on, or practice self-denial, we must place a high value on maturity.

Disruptive Discipleship aims to show you how to grow up—and how to do so on purpose.

WHAT YOU CAN EXPECT AND WHAT I CAN HOPE

In part one (chapters one through three), I'll tell stories about people who got stuck. You'll do a bit of personal assessment to see where you might need to mature, too. And you'll learn three experience-based approaches to help with your discipleship. Then you'll focus on asking good questions to convert one of those approaches into action. Without a bit of reflection on the front end, you may have trouble justifying the insertion of artificial hardships—designed experiences—into your life.

Part two (chapters four through six) explores the power of experiential discipleship to impact your maturity in three critical areas of growth. You'll spend one chapter on developing faith, another on hope, and a third on love. These three aren't the only virtues, but they are prime examples.

Part three (chapters seven through nine) addresses several application topics, including how to incorporate lessons from an experience into everyday living, how to deal with unwelcomed experiences (as well as Jesus' command to deny yourself when they come), and how to get stuck less often.

In addition to addressing those who feel stuck in their faith and want to get unstuck, I'll speak to those who wonder how to take Jesus more seriously. If this is you, Luke 9:23 probably poses a problem, because you want to take up your cross, but there's no obvious cross to take up. You're *already* living, giving, and loving faithfully. There is no real *cost* to your discipleship right now.[2] You aren't stuck, per se—just feeling underutilized. It could be unnecessary guilt causing the unrest, in which case I'd say, "Let it go." It could also be that life has settled into place well enough that you're finally seeing what was hidden in the busier times—namely, potential. The relative quiet has allowed Jesus' voice to come through: "Hey, friend, I've got more for you. Let's do this."

The other reader I'm thinking about is neither feeling stuck nor underutilized. For you, the challenge is transition. You've accepted a new job, you retired last month, you're graduating,[3] or you adopted a child. You've entered or are about to enter a new season—exciting or terrifying, minor or major—and you want to make the most of it.

Regardless of who you are or why you're here, none of us has reached maturity in Christ. For this reason, I want to thank you for joining me. Many of the stories I'll tell come from my own journey of success and failure along the way to maturity, and it means a lot to share them with you.

Notice that I said "along the way." I have certainly not arrived, and I have no fantasy that you will arrive by means of these pages. In fact, our patterns as humans are so New Year's Resolution–like that my words may serve only as one more prophetic inspiration: convicting yet short-lived. That's not a bad thing; it's just a normal, honest thing that proves the need for subsequent and repeated messages. How will we grow in faith, hope, and love if not by persistent prodding? We need fresh reminders.

With enough of these reminders, I'm convinced we can experience an ongoing life of discipleship, of being Jesus' students, in which we become more like him and grow more mature with each passing year. Lulls will come; hiccups will come. But they don't have to stop us.

If what you read here creates a spark, even a small one, do something about it. My wife enjoyed reading Ann Voskamp's *One Thousand Gifts* (Zondervan, 2010), but the real difference came when she took Ann's advice and filled a gratitude journal with a year's worth of entries. Likewise, I devoured Chip and Dan Heath's *Made to Stick* (Random House, 2008), but until I tested their advice in real instances of communication, the content had no place to stick. A book goes only so far without real-world application.

SUSPENDING NORMAL CAN BE SCARY. DISRUPTING ROUTINE CAN AND PROBABLY WILL CHANGE THE STATUS QUO. WHO CARES, IF IT MAKES US MORE LIKE CHRIST?

It was true in earlier times too: the Israelites received words from God but had to enter the desert for the words to take root. And Jesus was sent by the Father, but his calling had to be tested in the wilderness.

With a definitively experiential focus, *Disruptive Discipleship* will serve best if you take it beyond these pages. When Jesus said, "Come, follow me" (Matthew 4:19), the first disciples were able to physically get up and see where he would take them. Without that luxury today, we turn to activities that create a similar space for him to work.

Suspending normal can be scary. Disrupting routine can and probably will change the status quo. Who cares, if it makes us more like Christ? If an experience leaves you and me with a more patient faith, a more resilient hope, and a more selfless love for our neighbors, then let's take the risk and sign up.

Part One

GROWING

RESTLESS

FEELING STUCK

FAITH

Allie, a student traveling with us, had already vomited three or four times, and we were only as many hours down the mountain. The bus had two levels, and the uncirculated heat on the second floor smothered us even more than the lack of oxygen. Most of the Peruvian passengers slept soundly, but we did not—Allie especially. I had dozed off for another few minutes when a muffled commotion across the aisle stirred me awake.

"Is everything okay?" I asked quietly.

One of the college students in our group of sixteen whispered, "Allie threw up again." She reached for a baggie from the travel attendant, who I hadn't seen standing beside me in the dark.

"Do you need anything?" I asked.

"No. Thanks, Sam. Just pray for her to get some relief."

I felt my way to the tiny bathroom in the back, holding each handrail as the bus careened around another mountainside curve. Nausea affected me too. We took turns going in there for the tiny window that slid open just enough to suck in a draft of cool air. Twice we had asked that the climate be adjusted, and the attendant politely refused.

We had been serving kids in an afterschool program, and Allie hadn't adjusted well to either the altitude or the food. It simply wasn't like home, she'd say. Now the seven-hour trip from eleven thousand feet above sea level to the edge of the Pacific Ocean threatened to break her. Heather and two others took turns pulling back her hair and offering hopeful words as they looked out into the night for an indication of morning.

My female coleader and medical point person, Steph, checked in with Allie, but only once and only long enough to assess the situation before returning to her seat up front to sleep. There was nothing more for her to do. Yet that particular interaction hurt Allie. It didn't matter that I sat across the aisle with my own medical certifications or that the girls stayed up to assist her for hours. It didn't matter that we prayed to God for comfort. What mattered was that on that midnight bus ride, 3,500 miles from home with yet another sick bag in hand, and isolated from healthy, fresh air and familiar language, Steph was the symbol of a mother for Allie, and Steph had just gone back to bed. Allie felt abandoned.

HOPE

When Jen lagged behind our hiking group in the Great Smoky Mountains of Tennessee, I asked if everything was okay. "Yes, everything's fine," she said. She didn't seem fine, so I asked again.

"I've got a little headache, that's all."

I went through a few of the questions I normally ask as a leader: How long have you had it? Does it feel like a typical headache? On a pain scale of one to ten, how bad is it? How much have you had to drink today? After all, our group would be a day's hike away from the van for the weekend, and little things can become big things quickly in a remote place, despite being just a few hours from the city.

Then I found the right question: "When was the last time you ate?"

"About four hours ago."

"Aren't you mildly hypoglycemic?" I asked.

"Yes."

"Do you think your headache is related to this?"

"Probably."

"Do you have any snacks on you?"

"I have a bag of M&M's in my backpack."

Meanwhile, we were continuing to hike along the trail, falling farther behind with each step.

"Do M&M's help your headache when your sugar is low?"

"Yes."

(Cue baffled tone.) "Well, *Jen*—we should get them out. Hold on while I tell the group to—"

Jen's nails dug into my arm. "Don't you dare," she pleaded. "I'm fine, and I'll get them out when we get to the campsite."

What was going on there? A valiant resolve to push through with the confident expectation that she would make it? Or a refusal of help because she didn't want to be exposed as weak to her peers?

LOVE

I heard my mother-in-law's voice downstairs, so I went down to say hello. As I entered the kitchen, I saw a dozen freshly baked pumpkin chocolate chip scones cooling on the table. The room smelled like every room should in the fall. And those scones were ours.

But Julie's mom had stopped by, and Julie was quick to tell her that she had been baking and "Here, you should take a couple for you and Dad." I love my mother-in-law, but my gut tightened at the offer, and I passed through the room.

A few minutes later, they asked for my opinion about this or that, and I glanced at the container in my mother-in-law's hand. We talked, and I stole another look, not quite able to get an accurate count of the scones in it. Back in the kitchen, I peeked again as we—the kids too—exchanged a few pleasantries and saw her out the back door.

She's a lovely woman. Easy to be around, caring, playful, the kind of person who makes you believe you're her best friend. She even bakes a special cake for me at Christmas, just because she knows I like it. But the second I closed the door behind her, I asked Julie why she had given her mom three, not two, scones. It came out in a light-hearted, passive-aggressive way, matching (superficially, at least) the mood of the house at the moment: singing children, dinner on its way to the table, and the lingering smell of the remaining scones. "Mom is having somebody over tonight," she replied.

I concentrated on the little twist in my stomach and tried to assess how to be generous while also honest about my disappointment. I couldn't think of anything, so we sat down at the table. I began to pray out of habit, "Lord, thank you for all that you provide—" and then, like a good boy, I inserted, "and please help me to be generous."

I couldn't continue. I rushed an amen and blurted to the family, "I don't actually want to pray that!"

The girls laughed in surprise, and I went on, saying mostly to Julie, "I don't feel generous right now, and I don't even *want* to be generous. And here's the irony: I came down the steps this evening thinking about Emma's new braces and how we'll all have to cut back in various ways in order to pay for them and how we should talk at dinner about seeing this as an opportunity to bless Emma because that's what families do—we sacrifice for each other. And then you went ahead and gave away the scones. Our scones. *My* scones! I felt so generous and in a flash so *not* generous."

At that point, eleven-year-old Alice, still laughing and also over-looking my quandary, jumped in. "Yeah, Mom, you're always giving away our scones." Yes, I was whining like a little brat, and yet the conflict was real to me.

Then I remembered something Julie did when her mom was in the kitchen: she paid her mom twenty dollars for a wedding shower gift they purchased together. (Her mom covered the bigger portion, by the way.) I remembered this and asked, "When you gave your mom that twenty dollars, I didn't bat an eye. But the scones—why did that make me angry?"

HOW CAN YOU BE SO BLIND?

Jesus often asked, in one manner or another, "How can you be so blind?" When the disciples huddled together to try to make sense of the parable of the four soils in Mark 4, the meaning seemed plain enough, but Jesus had to spell it out for them in detail.

And when Jesus cautioned them in Matthew 16 against the "yeast of the Pharisees and Sadducees" (v. 6), and the disciples thought he was referring to them forgetting to take bread along for the trip, he had to ask, "How is it you don't understand that I was not talking to you about bread?" (v. 11). I imagine being right there with them in their blindness. I hear him, but I don't get what he's saying.

As frustrating as it can be, this is one of the genius points about the Son of God—and one of the chief approaches he employed to get people unstuck. Throughout the Gospels, he behaved and spoke in a way that disrupted his listener's routine. *Leave your nets, heal the sick, come down immediately, go make disciples. Who do you say I am? Whose portrait is this? You give them something to eat.* Over and over, he pushed people into the open, where their blindness could be exposed. (See appendix A: "What Jesus Knew About Experiential Education.")

Did the response he often received cause his face to contort in frustration or his eyebrows to raise in bewilderment? The disciples couldn't have understood as he did, so I tend to believe he was less

exasperated than compassionate about their plight, though it had
to be difficult for him to have perfect clarity and simultaneously
surround himself with people who either couldn't see or weren't
willing to see. I think of friends who work as emergency room
doctors and face a particular lot of patients every weekend. These
caregivers ask themselves, *When will you realize that this food dis-
order will have you back in here again? When will you understand
that drinking this hard is going to kill you?*

When I was fifteen, I found an aluminum lawn chair in the woods
behind my grandfather's house. I assumed by its condition that it
was being discarded, so I asked Grandpa if I could carry it to the
trash pile. He said, "Sammy, there's nothing wrong with that chair."

I responded with what I saw as the obvious: "But it's out in the
woods, the metal is corroding, and the only webbing left is where
it's attached to the frame. And the little pieces of webbing that *are*
still attached have completely rotted."

He sat up proudly, as he had learned to do as the child of a once-
upstanding family—chest out, chin high—and said with perfect
diction, "That is a fine chair. And when we are able, we will have
new material fitted to it."

Maybe, I thought as someone old enough to understand restoration, *but not here and not by you.*

My grandfather had spent most of the previous four decades
wasting away in his parents' homestead, a nineteen-room house full
of antiques, oak floors, chandeliers, and French doors in the middle
of a hundred acres of prime real estate. He had been spoiled as a
kid and had made enough mistakes since then to make it impossible
for him to live anywhere but in the past.

Roof leaks were addressed with buckets. Falling plaster rested
in tarps nailed to the walls. His deceased daughter's Toyota Co-
rolla had sunken slowly into the yard for the previous twenty years,
untouched by anyone but me, who would sit in it and pretend to

be a race car driver until summer got hot enough to awaken the wasps.

And there was Grandpa's wig, purchased at a flea market so long ago that the hairs had clumped together, revealing the netting beneath. In all my life, I had not seen a single item fixed or replaced by this man. When money did come in from the occasional sale of an antique, it went to the horse track or to keep creditors at bay.

Even at fifteen, I couldn't understand the logic behind keeping that chair. It was clear that nothing would ever be done about it, if only because there were so many other, more important items requiring attention, like the hairpiece, which was so ratty that his two grown sons teased him incessantly about it.

Yet his straight-backed pride suggested a deep ignorance of the truth. He had been a musician, after all, raised to appreciate the finer things in life. The lawn chair was a symptom of his condition, and it reveals a few dangerous characteristics of being stuck.

Being stuck often goes unnoticed. When my sisters and I were in grade school, Mom stopped at the Shop 'n Save and asked me to run in for a jar of grape jelly. I balked with a litany of excuses: "*I* don't know how to buy *jelly*! I mean, there's *preserves*—who knows what *those* are—and *jam*, and other kinds with *seeds.*" Fluctuations in pitch accentuated my whining. "And there's so many *brand names*, and *sizes* of jars, and—"

"Okay, fine!" she said. "Jessica, will you go in? He doesn't know what to do, and I've got to stay here with the baby." Jessica shot fire at me and slammed the door. I was ten or eleven and already pretty good at getting my way.

It wasn't until I turned twenty-seven and worked in a university office that I was diagnosed by the department secretary. I had asked her for more pencils. She stood up, put on her heaviest tone of sarcasm, and patronizingly walked me—holding my hand—to the supply closet just feet away from her desk. She explained to me what paper is, what an eraser does, what pencils look like, and how I could pick them up with my very own fingers. We laughed, and then she said with seriousness, "Do you know what your problem is, Sam? You've got a bad case of learned helplessness."

She was right.

Being stuck often goes unnoticed. What negative patterns are so familiar to you that the comfort they produce desensitizes you from seeing them? How long has it been since you asked someone to speak into your life?

Being stuck affects every area of our lives. After my grandfather and father passed, I inherited a few remaining boxes of papers. Truckloads had been hauled away after Grandpa died and before the state came to repossess the house. Dad had held on to a few boxes for sentimental reasons. In them I found an unpaid gas bill for ten thousand dollars. It was dated from around the time I discovered the lawn chair in the woods, and it revealed the accumulating effect of delinquency. With each new piece of evidence, the picture was becoming clear: from the crumbling chimney to the cracked foundation, from broken

> **WHAT NEGATIVE PATTERNS ARE SO FAMILIAR TO YOU THAT THE COMFORT THEY PRODUCE DESENSITIZES YOU FROM SEEING THEM?**

relationships with his would-be heirs to disintegration in his artificial hair, the extent of Grandpa's state of being touched everything.

"'Are you still so dull?' Jesus asked [the disciples]. 'Don't you see that whatever enters the mouth goes into the stomach and then out of the body? But the things that come out of the mouth come from the heart, and these defile them" (Matthew 15:16-18). To the Pharisees, he said, "You are like whitewashed tombs, which look beautiful on the outside but on the inside are full of the bones of the dead and everything unclean" (Matthew 23:27). These responses seem harsh, even impatient. Yet as I know them to be true about my own life—not just Grandpa's— I hear them spoken as an attempt to get us unstuck in the deepest ways.

At the dinner table, I asked Julie why giving away those scones made me angry. She thought for a moment and replied, "It probably has to do with your snack panic."

The girls laughed again, because they know my habit of keeping a snack nearby, especially when I'm away from the house. It's like a security blanket, and it goes back to my childhood, when we didn't have enough to eat. I won't begrudge God of what he provided and how that provision came to us. But I always needed more. As a teenager, growing tall and playing sports, I could have only half a bowl of cereal for breakfast with even less milk. (If the cereal floated, I'd have to show Mom that it only *looked* like too much.) It wasn't Mom's fault. She was raising four of us by herself, and we often wondered how food would find our cupboards.

So I developed more than a simple snack panic all those years ago. The anger at the table was about the lingering fear that something special, something extra, something beyond what the old WIC check allowed was disappearing before I could enjoy it.

In a sense, I couldn't afford to be generous, because in the formative years of eight and ten and thirteen, money may have been my mom's issue, but what the money couldn't buy was my issue. That night, because of a few scones, it came back. Full cupboards, a secure job, an intact family, and still, buried beneath piety and the appearance of Christian charity, I had snarled at someone I love.

Being stuck affects every area of our lives. Are you willing to give Jesus unfiltered access to your life? Do you have the courage to say to a friend, "I might have an issue, but I'm not sure. Would you help me identify it?" Can you unpry your hands from the thing you love but that also keeps you bound?[1] Do you believe that Jesus cares about you through and through?

BEING STUCK AFFECTS EVERY AREA OF OUR LIVES.

THE POWER OF FEAR

Fear poses a significant threat to our growth in Christ. Despite years of provision and generosity, the experience of not having enough still affects my ability to be generous. I'm afraid there won't be enough. Cognitive therapist Dr. Michael Hurd writes, "People who have a certain bad set of experiences, if they fail to look at those experiences introspectively and objectively, tend to keep repeating those experiences and going towards what they know—not what's good for them, but what they know."[2]

What fear do you think Peter had when he denied knowing Jesus in John 18? Did it stem from childhood? It seems to appear again in Galatians 2:12. Was Jesus' questions to him in John 21:15-17 ("Do you love me?") an invitation to introspection so that Peter wouldn't keep repeating those experiences?

Getting unstuck can seem impossible. Maybe my grandfather was more aware of the situation than I gave him credit for. It's possible that he was completely ignorant of how stuck he was, though my observations and firsthand stories from relatives and friends of the family contradict this idea. As an intelligent man who was also proud (and therefore less likely to admit his shortcomings), he likely knew what a mess he was in, even if he couldn't admit it was his fault. Maybe he knew but couldn't see a way out.

Could he have said yes to throwing out the chair? Certainly, though it would have signified defeat. Telling himself he'd eventually refurbish what amounted to an inexpensive, recyclable item also meant that he could continue telling himself there would be money in the future to do it. And telling me I could trash it would mean surrendering a thread of hope—however unrealistic that hope might have been, especially since he never worked after his thirties.

And surrender he could not. As long as he lived, he would agree to whatever measure of self-deception promised to keep the dream alive. He had already lost the family business, the savings, and his marriage. Perhaps he refused to be the one who lost the house and its contents as well.

What do you do when it feels impossible to get unstuck? What do you have to tell yourself in order to live in your present state? In *I Told Me So: Self-Deception and the Christian Life*, Gregg Ten Elshof writes, "We can't bring ourselves to say that we have no intention to make significant and noticeable progress toward Christlikeness. But neither do we find ourselves simply doing the things of Jesus."[3]

DISRUPTING THE ROUTINE

Everybody gets stuck. For Allie on the bus in Peru, it was both literal (she physically couldn't escape her situation) and relational (her mother was, perhaps for the first time in Allie's life, absent). In that moment, this young woman experienced a crisis of faith: *Can the God she claimed to follow actually take care of her?* Mom had always provided, counseled, supported, and nursed, which meant this was new territory. Suddenly Allie found herself in a bigger pinch than she'd ever known, and not only was Mom missing, but Mom's stand-in—Steph—was sleeping. Allie was forced into a position to choose to entrust herself to God, who she could not see.

If Allie's issue involved faith—the belief that God *can*—then Jen's involved hope—the belief that God *will*. When I pushed for Jen to let me help her get those M&M's, she said through tears, "I don't want to be the one responsible for stopping the group. I'm just being a baby." So this was not about M&M's and hypoglycemia. Nor was it about avoiding undue attention from others, though that gets closer to the problem. Fundamentally, it was about *protection* from those others: *would she still be loved if her weakness was exposed?*

If we believe that God loves unconditionally, no exposure or threat of exposure should cause fear. This is far easier stated than followed, obviously. We (me included) tend to behave like the exiles in Jeremiah 44:15-18, who turned to a god that coincided with low risk. When we believe our prayers are being ignored, we grow impatient and look to other sources.

WHEN WE BELIEVE OUR PRAYERS ARE BEING IGNORED, WE GROW IMPATIENT AND LOOK TO OTHER SOURCES.

If faith is the belief that God can, and hope is the belief that God will, when I failed to love my mother-in-law, I failed to demonstrate those beliefs through action. I didn't love my neighbor as myself.

You can see that these three vignettes overlap. All three characters had issues with all three gifts. Just consider how a lack of faith and hope caused a lack of love in each of us: Allie didn't talk to Steph for days, even after Allie's health improved and even after Steph made attempts to reconcile. Jen shut off potential care from her community when she chose to hide her need. And I wanted those scones back, particularly the third one, but my mother-in-law was in the way, so I turned against her.

The point, then, is less about the details of how or why we're stuck than about *recognizing that we are stuck*. It's important just to acknowledge our reality. That sort of honesty is critical.

Naming a thing is the first stage in taking away its power. In some cases, this can be easy. Often it is not. How do I name what I cannot see—or cannot see clearly? Do I have to go to Peru for three weeks to discover that I lack faith? Do I need a counselor to point out my issues? Do I need someone to take what's valuable to me in order to confront my conditional love? Maybe.

I can say this: unless you are peculiarly gifted in self-analysis, and you practice reflection on a regular basis, *and* you have enough humility to let others speak truth into your life, it's possible that you will never discover where you're stuck unless something disrupts your routine.

So disruption is key.

Allie was stuck on a bus, but physically so were Steph and the rest of our group. Yet none of us experienced what Allie did. The bus scenario was only a catalyst for her. Being sick, trapped, and alone on another continent was not her real problem, however—as we saw. In fact, within a couple of days, her situation had so greatly improved that her acute pain had disappeared altogether. But that moment on the bus was special, because it opened her eyes to see that she had been stuck for years in the belief that her mom was enough.

Just as the headache was not Jen's real problem and giving away scones was not my real problem, these kinds of specific moments in time and space serve as aids to make us aware of the deeper ways we need help. Disruptions of routine help us see the taken-for-granted assumptions and limitations in that routine.

WILLY-NILLY?

The concept of disruption has roots in family therapy. The observation was that a family develops patterns that, over time, lead to stagnancy. Therapists would disrupt these patterns to make room for new patterns, believing that simply removing an old pattern would make room for good to emerge.

But does good automatically emerge? According to marriage and family therapist Paul Johns, disruption needs direction. "A tree can certainly grow best when it has space and freedom to do so. But it can reach its fullest potential when it grows toward the sunlight; a path for which it was designed."[4] For Paul, a Christian, that path is toward Christ.

When Jesus invited the rich young ruler to follow him, he wasn't asking for something impossible (Luke 18:22). But it felt impossible for that guy—because that guy already had his life in pretty good order. What's it like for those of us who also struggle with pride? Or fear? Or regret, guilt, or insecurity? Try asking King Herod to deny Salome's request in front of a crowd (see Mark 6:26). He wouldn't. He didn't. He liked John the Baptist, but he liked being liked even more. He was stuck.

Too often we remain stuck because we live in a mix of faithlessness and faith. We feel hopeless and hopeful simultaneously. We refuse love and yet also extend it in one breath. In other words, we've got enough of the good to make us okay with the bad. Life is like this: vibrancy and stagnancy, renewal and atrophy, all sharing the same space, which means it's normal to be somewhere along the continuum. How will we know whether our faith, hope, and love are closer to alive and free than dead and stuck? We need to test them. We need to step into new moments that reveal our current status and trajectory. These moments—designed experiences—offer more than we expect and often take us to places we did not expect.

Going somewhere unknown requires courage to admit there is somewhere to go to that is *not here*. Courage also helps us admit that Jesus is talking to us, not just to first-century listeners, when he asks, "How can you be so blind?" And courage enables us to name the ignorance or insecurity—or whatever has us stuck—so we can begin to move toward a maturity that reflects being a disciple of Christ, the very thing Allie was eventually able to do. Disruptions can open our eyes, and I'll say more later about what sight has done for her.

However small the portion of faith, hope, and love we discover in ourselves, we recognize it as a gift from God. Imagine, then, what can happen when we acknowledge the ways this gift has been underused and also confess the ways it has been misused. It will take courage. We won't be thriving at a higher level yet (Jesus has work to do and so do we), but we can grow because we're on our way.

EXPLORING OPTIONS 2

A Journeying Prayer

Jesus, take me once again on a journey.
Take me to the city,
Take me to the valley and to the mountain,
Take me to the desert.
Take me to the place of wandering,
The place of hunger,
The place of solitude and of pain.
Take me to the place where You seem so far away
Yet only You are there.
Remove my crutches of possessions,
Remove the pillars of my faithless life,
Remove all the thumbs I suck.
And there in that place where nothing is left,
There refine my soul.
Amen.

Andy Freeman and Pete Greig, *Punk Monk*

I had an older cousin who liked to pin me to the ground and tickle me until I couldn't breathe. I hated it, but I was too small to escape. I wasn't just stuck; I was trapped. Seconds away from peeing my pants, I wanted more than anything to be free, but I had no solution until one providential day when I devised a plan. I realized that if I couldn't get out of this torture, I'd try to push through it. The next time her family came over, I veered too close, and down to the earth I went. Only this time, I gave no response. She dug deeper. Still nothing. I just stared at her. What she didn't know was how terribly I suffered behind that stare, but I could not—would not—satisfy my tormenter. And do you know what happened? She quit. I was no fun to tickle, so she turned back into the cousin I enjoyed being around.

> **I DON'T SEEK CHANGE UNTIL I REALLY WANT CHANGE.**

I learned a valuable lesson: I don't seek change until I really want change. In this case, I really wanted it. It hurt to persevere—I thought for sure I'd crack. But I was tired of being stuck, and the short-term hurt was far better than the long-term torture.

DESIGNED EXPERIENCES

One of the most effective ways to pursue maturity in faith, hope, and love is by disrupting routine on purpose. Natural causes and tragedy push us further, but we have no control over that realm. For those who have cushier lives, it could be a long wait for growth to appear, since ease is not very productive.

The alternative is to design an experience—an out-of-the-ordinary activity that gets us unstuck and promotes lasting growth. Mark Scandrette writes, "Rock-bottom, near-death and Damascus-road experiences are gifts, some of the many ways that God initiates transformation in our lives. But we've also been given the ability to imagine, plan and set direction, choose our objectives, and order our activities according to vision, values and goals."[1]

Reflecting on Matthew 18:8 and Jesus' advice to cut off your hand if it gets you in trouble, Scandrette claims that "the underlying message is clear: we should do whatever is necessary to face our shadows and brokenness."[2]

There are many ways to do this, with benefits to boot. Designs are easy to come by, easy to modify, and available at any age. And because they vary in purpose, shape, length, cost, intensity, and location, they include a wide range of activities, from restoring an antique to restraining from coffee, from singing a solo to serving overseas. Regardless of the details, a good design should contain enough discomfort and risk to cause us to bite our lip in anticipation—at least a little—like when the urban college student refused to backpack with me by saying, "Sam, I'll spend a week in the forest with you if you'll spend a week in the hood with me." That would have caused lip biting for both of us.[3]

In one example, I remember seeing the equipment list for a cave rescue training course. I had spent years in the wilderness and at least some time in caves, but I was a relative novice, and the list left me with many questions: When it says "3 pr. non-cotton socks," does it mean warm socks? How long will we be in the cave? Will I need to carry them with me to change if one pair gets wet? How can I tell if they're made of cotton? What if they are only 50 percent cotton?

And there were another two dozen items on the list! The training course, although related to my field of expertise, was foreign enough that I couldn't even feel confident about socks.

Anticipation like this meant I was heading into a new place. I couldn't predict what the experience would do to me or whether I would fail or succeed at the course work or in the eyes of peers who seemed relaxed about the whole thing. In short, I was scared.

Discomfort and risk make us vulnerable, exposing weaknesses we didn't know we had as well as ones we know we have but try to hide. God can work with scared. As Dave on the cartoon series

Scaredy Squirrel says, "Darkness is just the friend you can't see."[4]
Designed experiences put us there on purpose. They make us say,
"Okay, God, I said yes just now, but I'm wishing I had said no. I could
still say no, but I don't think I should. Will you meet me here?"

It's important to note that getting unstuck is not the end goal.
Maturity is more than reversing a temporary, negative trend; it represents a lifelong pursuit of wholeness. Faith, hope, and love are
endless attributes and always positive. The more we have of them,
the healthier we become, and the more our humanness can reflect
the image of God.

> "OKAY, GOD, I SAID YES JUST NOW, BUT I'M WISHING I HAD SAID NO. I COULD STILL SAY NO, BUT I DON'T THINK I SHOULD. WILL YOU MEET ME HERE?"

I want to offer three types of designs for pursuing this kind
of maturity. Each has its own way of addressing an old thing by introducing a new thing, and
each addresses being stuck. They all involve disrupting routine.
At least one should resonate with your particular need.

I. DIAGNOSTIC DESIGNS

It's hard to know what we need. I agree that "we should do whatever
is necessary to face our shadows and brokenness," as Scandrette
wrote, but shadows and brokenness can be tough to name since
they exist in our routine. My sister Holly tells a funny yet sad story
about a classmate who turned to say good morning, and Holly
gagged in her face. When the girl, concerned, asked if she was okay,
Holly didn't have the heart to tell her that her breath stank terribly.
How could the girl not know? Denial? Familiarity? She seemed to
be unaware as much as we are unaware that the house is cluttered
or that we have a drinking problem. I think of our shadows and
brokenness like halitosis, which lingers unnoticed until you get too
close. They're all part of our lives. Diagnostic designs cause us to
see them.

Signing up for a new experience without knowing exactly why it's needed is like having an annual physical—it reveals if and where we're stuck. (I didn't need this type of design while pinned under my cousin. I knew exactly what was going on.) From taking a workout class to teaching Sunday school, diagnostic designs are open-ended and include a wide range of unfamiliar experiences. The key is treating them, well, diagnostically—letting each new experience reveal what it may and then paying attention to what it produces.

Take volunteering at a soup kitchen. You can sign up and be of great help even if you aren't interested in self-exploration. With a diagnostic approach, however, you sign up but also pay attention. You take note of unusual internal responses, such as fear or sadness. You watch for surprising behaviors (your own, of course), such as avoiding eye contact. If you wash your hands more vigorously than normal, ask, "Why? What am I so worried about?" You might uncover an important truth. Paying attention is central to this design type and should begin when you first sign up and continue after the experience has ended. Here are a few sample questions that may come from paying attention.

Before you volunteer:

- "I'm really excited. Is it because I'll be volunteering with my friend? If I didn't have a résumé to strengthen, would it matter as much?"
- "I told them I'd go, but I don't want to. Is it from fear of losing a Saturday or because I'll be working with strangers?"

While you volunteer:

- "My heart breaks when I see women pass through the line, but not when the men do. What's going on?"
- "I seem to enjoy the breaks more than the work. Am I tired? Uncomfortable?"

After you volunteer:

- "I feel guilty. Is this emotional guilt? Privilege guilt?"
- "The hours went so fast, and I was sad when the day ended. What does that mean moving forward?"

These observations stem from basic reflection, and basic reflection comes from asking questions. The key element in each of these questions is paying attention to emotions, particularly (but not always) negative emotions. Perhaps you feel more comfortable behind the counter than when mingling with guests, which makes you wonder if it's not introversion as you suspected but something more like prejudice. Now you've got content to address. Paying attention creates space for discipleship to occur even on a random Saturday in March.

What if you volunteer *every* Saturday? If the experience is not so out-of-the-ordinary, can it still be diagnostic? Sure. Instead of "What am I experiencing in this new place?" the question becomes "What patterns do I see in my weekly role? What keeps me from being uncomfortable in my routine?"

Imagine that I enjoy working with the people who come each weekend. I serve them and listen to their stories, as I've done for years. One day I decide to pay attention during my shift. I ask God to help me listen to what's happening inside, and I approach the day with curiosity and a posture of receptivity. This turns the day into a diagnostic experience. Same clothes, same warm smile—different approach.

Hours in, I make a peculiar observation. It's not new, now that I think about it, but odd, as though I'm seeing it for the first time: conversations with guests are one-sided—in their favor. I'm there to serve, after all. But it brings to mind the director's request that volunteers maintain relative anonymity. I like this request. (Or is it a rule?) When I explore why, I wonder if it makes it easier to have conversations here. I don't have to get into the deep stuff of my own life. Everyone knows the director's request, so it's expected that I withhold personal information. And that's when I make a discovery, a diagnosis: I don't have to be known here. *Nobody can hurt me here.* My service is—to one extent or another—a hiding place that allows me to maintain control and go on believing I am the hands and feet of Jesus (which I am) while at the same time avoiding what those hands and feet want to do for me.

Self-protection is insular—from ourselves, from others, and even from God. Engaging with the deeper whys behind a commitment to that kitchen helps me see beyond the gift of generosity to the fear of intimacy. Now I've got content to address.

For all that can be learned at a soup kitchen, it's relatively low-risk. The work is predictable enough for me to explore stuck spots without taking many chances, which protects me from being stretched to a lip-biting degree. It is a rather controlled growth environment. But what about settings that surpass our control, settings that decrease predictability and increase risk? Those can be diagnostic as well. Much more so, in fact.

When Allie signed up to spend those three weeks in Peru with three leaders and twelve other students from eight different universities, she had no idea what role a sweltering bus in the night would play. All she knew was that going to a faraway place would open an unusual space for growth. That in itself was an act of faith—a diagnostic approach to discipleship. She believed God would meet her there, and it didn't matter if he did so in big ways or small. The mere act of signing up required enough courage that she couldn't imagine him *not* meeting her.

Why would she have felt that way? Because nothing was familiar about it. Had she volunteered at the soup kitchen, it would be close to home. She might recognize the guests, and she would understand their language. If anything bad happened, her familiarity with

the culture—how to communicate with emergency personnel, how
to read street signs—would permit her to get help or go home with
confidence. The amount of faith demanded in comfortable circumstances is far less than what's needed in unfamiliar territory.

**THE AMOUNT OF FAITH DEMANDED
IN COMFORTABLE CIRCUMSTANCES
IS FAR LESS THAN WHAT'S NEEDED
IN UNFAMILIAR TERRITORY.**

In XD, we refer to this as
"suspending normal." For Allie,
this is what happened: we
lifted her out of her daily
routine, transported her to a
foreign setting (completely foreign, as far as she was concerned),
and set her down with the expectation that she get along as usual.
We suspended her normal. When I say *we*, I mean, of course, that
she gave us permission. We explained what we planned to do, invited her to come along, and then she, having understood the risks
enough to know she would need to relinquish control, said, "Yes,
sign me up."[5]

You can grasp, then, why her experience was so eye opening
compared to what she was used to. She needed more interdependence than self-reliance. She needed a translator to assist with basic
needs. She needed to ask what was on her plate and if the water was
safe and if her migraine would fade as she acclimated to the altitude
or if she would need to see a doctor. Despite the similarities (she
ate, slept, walked, and talked, just like at home), nothing was the
same. In fact, excessive stimulation and interpretation complicated
the act of paying attention. The traumatic bus ride and Allie's subsequent emotional reaction to Steph only muddled what reflective
clarity Allie might have had in an already clouded moment. It took
a restful environment, a return to physical health, multiple reconciliation attempts, long conversations, and continued spiritual work
after the trip for Allie to recognize how stuck she had been.

Do I regret inviting Allie to participate? Absolutely not. It's a
beautiful thing to see her now. Her work as an event planner involves

dealing with surprises and knowing when she needs help and when she doesn't. And she works in a collaborative environment where others care about her growth in Christ. Diagnostic designs promote this kind of growth.

2. PRESCRIPTIVE DESIGNS

The second type of design is a bit of the opposite. Prescriptive designs require knowing or at least having a sense of what the problem is and then signing up for an experience that addresses it. These tend to be responsive, even reactive. For example, you spend Ash Wednesday reflecting on the cost of Jesus' ministry and praying to know what you need, when it becomes clear that screen time is an issue. You've got too many devices with too many apps lit up for too many hours each day, and you're stuck in a pattern of dependence on them. That's the diagnosis. So you design a prescriptive experience by deciding to unplug the TV for Lent. (More in chapter three on my own media awakening.)

If diagnostic designs are open-ended and full of surprises, prescriptive designs offer specific solutions. They are like what their name entails: filling a prescription at a pharmacy. The medicine may work or it may not, but based on the diagnosis, it's the best way to counter the symptoms that you know of.

Reacting. Speaking of medicine, prescriptive designs often follow a health scare. You get your cholesterol checked, and the next day you're downloading a couch-to-5k running app and hitting the road in new sneakers. This reaction may appear to have little to do with faith, hope, and love, but it is prescriptive nonetheless. It proves that you care about *not* dying of a heart attack. Even self-focused care can convert into a purpose larger than yourself, like realizing family and clients depend on you being alive.

Prescriptive designs also follow personal frustration, like when the cap of the staircase newel post comes off in your hand again.

Unlike Clark Griswold in *National Lampoon's Christmas Vacation*, who took the chainsaw to it, or George Bailey in *It's a Wonderful Life*, who simply put it back, you decide then and there to fix everything broken in your life. It is that last straw that clarifies the real problem: you and your chronic procrastination; your persistent fear of never amounting to anything; your lack of handyman experience; your chaotic schedule. Something within pronounces a New Order, and immediately you watch a DIY video and cash in the gift card buried in the sock drawer. You're on a mission to conquer the newel post—and (released hero that you are) the rest of the staircase too.

Whatever finally grabs your shirt collar and shakes you—the dog peeing on the rug, the neighbor smoking outside your bedroom window—impulsivity is the catalyst for many prescriptive designs. However catalyzing it may be, reaction isn't the best route. There's no lengthy reflection or search for second opinions, just a pinprick realization that you've been stuck for too long. One thing is certain: prescriptive awakenings benefit from suddenness because they eliminate time for your old mind to talk you out of it with *You don't know what you're doing* and *Can't you see what this will cost?* You're already in the car with a new mind leading the way.

Reflecting. Impulsivity may get you going, but pausing to simmer generates two beneficial buttresses of sustainability: a better plan and a better motive.

First, reflection gives reaction a better plan. With the newel post, taking time to ask around leads to borrowing tools you thought you'd have to buy, and the money saved becomes enough to pay an electrician to rewire the staircase light. A better plan also leads to scheduled time off, buy-in from a spouse or roommate, and fewer do-overs. Reflection is maturity at work.

Second, reflection gives reaction a better motive. Tackling a project to prove that your parents have misjudged you will result only in disappointment. Maybe the newel post needs to be fixed, but insecurity should have nothing to do with it. Nor should pride or peer pressure. Pausing gives time for closer matches between symptoms and prescriptions, like doing the job out of generosity to the landlord.

The point is to convert bad habits into good habits. If you finished the staircase but did so reactively, the odds of reverting to bad habits are high. Then who cares if you finished? Wake-ups are rare, generous gifts. If another one doesn't come around for a while, you could end up like *Napoleon Dynamite's* Uncle Rico, talking about that one time years ago when you were something in high school.

You need sufficient space to reflect, to pray, to seek wisdom—all of which leads to better plans and better motives. And yet you don't want to lose the reactive energy experienced in that gift of an awakening moment. It's the balance between "look before you leap" and "he who hesitates is lost."

There is a significant upside to designing an experience: other people. What begins internally—by the Holy Spirit's prompting or some other conviction to step out in faith—often ends disappointingly when we neglect community involvement. We may be capable of swallowing a horse pill to address an illness. We may even have the rare fortitude to manage the entire dosage cycle alone. But the Lord understands our trouble with self-sustainability, and he complements many designs with outside aid.

As Kyle Idleman describes so well, the prodigal son acts, but he does not possess the power to act *completely*.[6] "And so he got up" is the simple indication Jesus makes of the young man's initial response to being stuck. It is the young man's *father* who restores him to full health (Luke 15:20). Like the son, we often need someone to meet us as far as we've managed to come and help us make it the rest of the way. We need the Father, and we need flesh-and-blood helpers in our everyday journey toward maturity. For they are what we are not: an outside perspective, a standing-right-there objective voice. And they play this role because they know us and have permission to play it. Their partnership increases the success of the design.

As a parent, I want my kids to glean from intergenerational wisdom, a desire sparked by my own parents, who made us visit nursing homes and grandparents for hours on end. It was the last place I wanted to be as a kid. Now, having neighbors who are older and homebound, I enjoy their company. When Harold up the street asks, "Would you like to sit down a while?" I say yes gladly.

How do I get my own kids to this place? I'm not as diligent as Mom was. So when our pastor asked recently that we sit in new locations during church on Sundays with people different from us in age, we took him up on the offer.

"A multigenerational expression doesn't pander to our preferences," he said gently. "It causes discomfort and challenges us to grow." Sounded like prescriptive design language to me. It wasn't a need at the urban Presbyterian church we attended years ago, but in this congregation, it was. And listen, it isn't only my kids who need this prompting. As honorable as it might seem that I call Harold now and then, I'm a guy who likes his preferences to be pandered to. I need others to help me grow.

3. PREPARATORY DESIGNS

Diagnostic designs are born from knowing we don't know what we need. Prescriptive designs respond to what we do know. The third approach to growing in faith, hope, and love begins with knowing that harder times will come.

When I turned thirty-five, I strained my back because I thought I could still play soccer like a fifteen-year-old. I hadn't prepared for it. I did zero core-strengthening exercises at that time, which meant I was more prone to injury. And the injuries I suffered took longer to heal.

Preparatory designs involve shoring up for the future by growing in stamina and resilience. If you stretch your faith by doubling your tithe while still young, by the time kids and economic downturns come, you'll be in a place of trust that God will provide. Preparation recognizes susceptibility to getting stuck before we actually get stuck.

In Luke 4, Jesus entered the desert to be tempted by the devil. God had chosen that environment and length to challenge others before, and it seems his reasons weren't all that different. A long period in an unforgiving location does something to us; perhaps it even breaks part of us.

Picture any desert: the Sahara, the Gobi, the Mojave. Picture spending two days there. By yourself. Overnight. With no gear, no food, no friends. No smartphone or hammock, either. How many hours pass before you want a granola bar and a tree to eat it under? Increase the length to a week. Three weeks. Still no granola bar. Still no hammock. And what about the eyes staring at you in the darkness? As Jesus spent forty days in the Judean wilderness—more wilderness than straight hot-sand desert—the conditions would have pushed him to the max.

I've seen enough survival shows like *Alone* to believe I could handle part of this challenge. It would be tougher than what Tom Hanks faced in *Cast Away*, but delusion and residual invincibility from my youth make the challenge sound do-able. Of course, fear is eased by the vision of a camera crew and emergency personnel, like Bear Grylls had in *Man vs. Wild*. Could I make it a week? Ten days? Far less with inclement weather. Louis Zamperini, the subject of Laura Hillenbrand's biography *Unbroken*, endured forty-seven days at sea.

The desert might have more resources. I could find a cave for shelter and track animals for food. I don't really know my capabilities when it comes to this level of endurance. Heck, I've never even attended the forty-day mountain experience my colleagues host for college students, and they carry high-tech gear and ingredients for pizza and a satellite phone to post updates on social media.

Fortunately, preparatory designs are not aimed to kill. Yes, they get us ready for scenarios and seasons that may seem unsurvivable. Yes, the thought of them might drain blood from our faces. But they aim for good—to fortify and to show what we're made of in a relatively controlled environment. As such, they prepare us for what lies beyond the wilderness, for a future none of us has access to.

"Remember how the LORD your God led you all the way in the wilderness these forty years, to humble and to test you in order to know what was in your heart, whether or not you would keep his commands" (Deuteronomy 8:2). Moses is clear that Israel's time in

JESUS AS DESIGN GUIDE

Consider these guidelines for preparation from Jesus' test in the desert.

1. *Preparation should relate to the future challenge, if possible.* If you exercise and I don't, and we both get hurt, you will probably recover sooner. That's because there is a direct correlation between preparation and challenge. There is also an indirect correlation. For example, a desert has nothing directly to do with Jesus' ministry, but it was perfect for challenges he would face.

- The desert is a lonely place. Jesus' work would require being alone when others misunderstood his theological and political views.

- The desert is an uncomfortable place. Jesus' work would require self-denial. Tiredness, contention, absence of trust, fickle companions, lack of progress—these awaken temptations toward self-indulgent escapism.

- The desert is a barren place. Jesus' work required that he waited for the Father to provide.

the desert was meant to see what the people were made of. He stated the objective of the test: "He humbled you, causing you to hunger and then feeding you with manna, which neither you nor your ancestors had known, to teach you that man does not live on bread alone but on every word that comes from the mouth of the LORD" (v. 3). If the people were to make it in real life, they needed specific preparation to get them there.

Beyond training for a race or investing in retirement—both of which have specific end dates—and beyond the general prediction

2. *Knowledge should inform the kind of preparation.* You study before a test. You drive a new car carefully until the engine breaks in. You definitely pay attention to your fiancée so you can make Valentine's Day a big deal like her parents always did, because their anniversary is on that same day, and they always gave their kids a special meal and gifts, and you don't ever want to screw it up like you did that first year together, when you treated it like any other day. Knowledge matters.

What did Jesus know that made him say yes to the desert experience? A lot. He was thirty. He lived in community. (Think of how community has taught us: through advisers directing class schedules, coaches fine-tuning biomechanics, pastors giving advice, parents teaching about failure.) Jesus also studied history. He understood the Law and had mingled with religious leaders since his youth. He also followed the political situation of his nation.

In short, at least on the fully human side, if Jesus didn't know everything, he certainly had a sense of what was coming. He knew the prep for his future would require more than a few all-night Scripture cramming sessions. He knew the training would need to match the intensity of the work ahead—challenges that would exceed any he'd encountered so far. So when the Spirit said, *We're going to the desert,* Jesus knew to say yes.

that says if you play sports you're likely to get hurt so you'd better work out, how do we prepare for the generic tomorrow when cancer appears or a parent disappears?[7] We invest in the principles that lie at the heart of the Scriptures and of every desiring follower of Christ: a mature faith, a mature hope, and a mature love.

This is not practical. Volunteering at a soup kitchen is practical. Abdominal crunches are practical. Investing in faith, hope, and love is not. Not immediately, at least. Chapters four through six will address that concern. For now, it's important—no, critical—to grasp the centrality of faith, hope, and love in preparation for what lies ahead. Growth in these three essentials builds a foundation for the storms to come. They won't prevent the storms. They won't keep the storms from causing damage. But they provide stability. They develop a strong core. They keep us grounded in periods of insecurity and free in periods of oppression. They give us room to be charitable when the cost is great. They make us more like Christ, who demonstrated reliance upon these same three, even as he had the advantage of knowing far more about his future than we do—a reason to take them all the more seriously.

Why is this necessary—this serious undertaking? Because some of us will, inevitably, face a job loss that questions our prowess, and we need to be ready with *faith* to believe that God can meet our needs. Some of us will finally admit that we lack the power to break a habit, and we need to be ready in that vulnerable moment to surrender in *hope*, believing that God will see us through with sufficient grace. Some of us will end up with a neighbor who makes our blood boil, and we need to be ready to put our faith and hope into action by loving that person as Christ would.

SAYING YES TO MORE

In the movie *The Princess Bride*, Westley tells Buttercup, "Life is pain, Highness. Anyone who says differently is selling something."

It sounds pessimistic, but we learn of Westley's true disposition when the two of them survive the fire swamp, a supposedly inescapable forest. When they exit, the enemy appears, and Westley declares, "Ah, but how will you capture us? We know the secrets of the fire swamp. We can live there quite happily for some time." This fractured fairy tale provides an example of what tests can do for us. Yes, Buttercup catches on fire and disappears in lightning sand, and Westley gets attacked by a Rodent of Unusual Size. But they also discover what they're made of, insight they would need in times to come.[8]

There are ways around the fire swamp, of course—we can waive insurance or ignore the leaking roof. But how many evasions benefit us? The apostle Paul proclaimed that "suffering produces perseverance; perseverance, character; and character, hope" (Romans 5:3-4). It's a painful progression, but look where it leads: to hope! The fact that Jesus entered this progression on purpose and calls us to do the same means we ought to take him seriously. Scandrette affirms this need to respond: "When we risk going to new places, meeting new people and risking new activities, the resulting disequilibrium can create space for change."[9]

Whatever Jesus knew, we know less. Whatever he could endure, we can endure less. But we aren't babies who live on pureed peas and carrots. We have experience, familial and cultural influences, vocation, weaknesses, self-awareness, and spiritual moxie. These inform us quite a bit. And we have a God who is faithful at prompting us if we're willing to listen. The exact path to maturity in Christ may be mysterious, but we can start, and that is something.

So begin at the beginning. Admit immaturity. Recognize that you cannot stay at your current maturity level. Then pick a direction: Do you need to diagnose, prescribe, or prepare? What fits best at this time?

Then sign up. Just make sure it's hard. Entertainment does not create disciples.

By considering a response at all, you are saying, "I'm living a B-minus life, and I'd like to make it a B-plus." That's a big deal. Take that half step in maturity with the right design. If volunteering at the soup kitchen would help, go for it. Google has the number.

However, that half step comes in a thousand marvelous shapes—more specific, more homemade—which means you need a more robust approach. Slapping a cut-and-paste experience into your calendar may do the trick, but a custom-fit design invites you into the process deeply, revealing insight you may not get any other way.[10] In chapter three, I want to tell you about a personalized design I implemented and about what good came of it. So let's polish your rough sketch and by God's grace launch your next season of growth.

ENTERTAINMENT DOES NOT CREATE DISCIPLES.

MAKING A PLAN

3

By February 2010, I had watched an embarrassing number of football games that season. I'm a Pittsburgh Steelers fan by birth and enjoy Sunday afternoon games when I can. But that year was out of control, especially with my team en route to the championship. One fine weekend after the next slipped away as I sank into the couch. Then as the Super Bowl clock hit zero and the Green Bay Packers celebrated a win, I scraped the bottom of my salsa bowl with one more corn chip and helped friends clean up their party. I drove home and unplugged the TV.

This wasn't a fundamentalist reaction to media guilt but a reaction to wasted time. Nor was it a reaction in the sudden sense of the word. It was a response that came from weeks of nagging questions: *What's happening? Why can't I pull away from these games? What's at stake if I keep this up?* Even before the playoffs, my situation felt like being caught in the trash compactor on the Death Star while the walls pressed in. Back then, the season was just starting to get good. I couldn't stop. *Star Wars* characters Leia,

Luke, Han Solo, and Chewbacca understood the urgency of their situation. I, on the other hand, figured I had time. In Kyle Idleman's terms, I was awakening to the problem, but I was not ready for honesty or action.[1]

Here's what I recognized as the questions appeared: (1) I'm a creator, a cultivator, and a caregiver of myself and of those things I've been given, and (2) I'm not attending to any of them.

Because I wasn't attending to these core aspects of my identity as a child of God, they were leaving their own depressions in the couch cushions. They sat like dogs waiting for their owner to take them for a walk, occasionally whimpering with a Newtonian reminder that a person watching too much football tends to continue watching football. I did, however, concede to one activity during repeat commercials and boring third quarters: I entertained questions. The louder the whimpers, the more questions I let through, until they began to reveal a truth about my situation: *the walls were closing in!*

It's incredible to be made in the image of God. Those parts that reflect him can't be ignored—not forever, at least. I can go for a while without heeding—a few days, maybe the better part of a season—but then that tiny reflection space lets them be noticed again, and I awaken with the desire to create or to rearrange resources to make something new again. That's when I see Jesus standing between me and the digital screen with the leashes in his hand. I grab them and the dogs and run for the door.

Every design, even one so apparently simple as fasting from TV, begins with asking questions. They start off generically: *What's going on here?* Then they multiply in numerous directions, exploring and analyzing, like when my coworker Peter called for advice on planning a weekend retreat for student leaders: "Who are the students?" I asked. "Why do you want a retreat? Why do *they* need a retreat? Do they know each other? Do you know them?

How well? What is their relationship with you? Are you an authority figure, a mentor, or a campus adviser assigned to oversee them? If they volunteered for a leadership role in your ministry, what attracted them to it? How invested are they in this retreat idea? Are they hungry for instruction or interaction? Do they prefer busy or quiet? What will your budget permit? Do you have transportation limitations? Are they believers? Would you like to be in the outdoors?"

You don't need an inquisition necessarily, but you do need more than a basic glance around the room.

QUESTIONS AND MORE QUESTIONS

Entertaining questions in the dull moments of my TV time wasn't novel. I like questions. I like to know why snails leave slime and what makes the crunching sound in my left knee. Questions appear whether I'm running on the trail or driving to the store, and they inhabit a significant portion of my professional life, as they did when Peter called.

Questions take us places. Speaking of Peter and his student leader retreat, after thirty minutes on the phone, I had enough information to offer a few suggestions. He ditched the first few but liked another, so I started an additional round of questions to build on it. We continued this back-and-forth collaborative cycle—questions for clarity, suggestions deleted and kept, new questions asked—until an hour had gone by. All the while, we had been moving incrementally from diagnosis to prescription. At last he said, "My brain is full. I've got enough notes to move ahead, and some of these ideas weren't on my radar. I'm even more excited to serve this group of students now." The questions were taking him places.

Questions break our routine. They're like strangers bearing gifts—we don't know exactly what they'll reveal. By default, asking

questions assumes we don't have answers. I could have given Peter
a retreat formula, but he wasn't interested in a cut-and-paste approach. He didn't want the equivalent of matching Christmas
neckties for Dad, Brother, and Grandpa. He wanted a gift that was
fitting and fruitful for his ministry. Peter wanted to encourage maturity, not add stuff to his students' calendars. The same is true for
a design you might be creating for yourself. Move beyond the one-
size-fits-all approach.

> **PETER WANTED TO ENCOURAGE
> MATURITY, NOT ADD STUFF
> TO HIS STUDENTS' CALENDARS.**

Questions let us look around
corners. Looking may lead to answers, but it may also lead to
more questions. One follows an-
other until we come to the *real* question—the one question we
couldn't have possibly known to ask ten questions ago. Perplexing
and incorrigible, they can just as easily knock our faith assumptions
off-balance because they can take us on a scavenger hunt with trea-
sures at the end.

What else do questions do? They pause the to-do train. For
those who favor productivity over process (or, to borrow language from wilderness orienteering, "distance over direction"),
questions challenge our assumptions: *Will the training event I
planned last year work again this year, or do my employees need
a new approach?*

Good designs thrive on questions, so ask a lot of them. Working
through the section "Five Questions Every Design Needs" below
will be sufficient for most, but if you're the type who enjoys a good
riddle ("Eight people are dead in a cabin on the side of a mountain.
What happened?") you may elect to keep going. If that's you, ask
questions you think you already have answers for. Ask questions
that seem unrelated. And if you ask a question that doesn't present
an answer, ask different questions until it does.

If it feels intimidating to ask questions out loud or you aren't sure how to go about it, consider the range of questions people asked Jesus when they wanted to grow:

"Teacher . . . what must I do to inherit eternal life?" (Luke 10:25)

When they wanted to frame him:

"Is it right for us to pay taxes to Caesar or not?" (Luke 20:22)

When they wanted to complain:

"Lord, don't you care that my sister has left me to do the work by myself?" (Luke 10:40)

When they were perplexed:

"Where could we get enough bread in this remote place to feed such a crowd?" (Matthew 15:33)

When they felt desperate:

"Lord, should we strike with our swords?" (Luke 22:49)

When they were self-serving:

"Who . . . is the greatest in the kingdom of heaven?" (Matthew 18:1)

What I love is the way Jesus' answers repeatedly surprised the questioners. The disciples' perplexity over feeding the crowd, for example, birthed a question they assumed was unanswerable, but Jesus surprised them. The spies who asked about paying taxes to Caesar were sure their question would frame this religious troublemaker, but Jesus surprised them. The young man seeking eternal life thought his question would fill in that last bit of missing righteousness, but Jesus surprised him too. Questions have the power to launch an adventure. So go ahead and ask.

THE QFT

The Question Formulation Technique, or QFT, is a tool to help generate questions.[2] It originated when parents didn't get involved in a dropout prevention program because they didn't know what questions to ask. Today it's used widely with groups. Here are the first five steps, which you can adapt for personal use or for helping a friend.

1. *Create a question focus*—for example, "I watch more TV than I used to."

2. *Stick to the rules for producing questions:*

   • Ask as many questions as you can.

   • Do not stop to discuss, judge, or answer any of the questions.

   • Write down every question exactly as it was stated.

   • Change any statements into questions.

3. *Produce questions.* See how many you can write in ten minutes.

4. *Improve the questions.* Turn closed-ended questions into open-ended questions—from "Is it bad to watch TV?" to "When is it bad to watch TV?"

5. *Prioritize the questions.* Pick three questions you really want to answer. My top question was "What's at stake if I keep watching this much TV?"

FIVE QUESTIONS EVERY DESIGN NEEDS

As promised, I want to fill in this process with a closer attention to detail. Custom designs tend to fit better, but they also require more work. I have a feeling you're going to like this kind of work. It should generate excitement in the same way that planning a much-needed trip can generate excitement, because it promises to move you from concepts and loose plans to reality.

You know you want to head out West, but when and with whom? For how long and with what kind of transportation? These are the details that actually take you places, and they begin with questions.

In chapter one, we looked at the first step of the design process: *naming the issue.* Is it complacency? Anxiety? Not enough financial self-discipline? Greed? Insecurity? Fear? Where are you stuck and how is it affecting your faith, hope, or love? (This is where the QFT can be helpful.)

Then I presented three ways to address the issue, which led to step two: *determining what type of experience you should design.* Diagnostic designs work well if you aren't sure what you need help with. Prescriptive can show where you're stuck and serve as a pry bar to get out. Preparatory can train you for the known *and* unknown challenges ahead.

With these first two steps underway, it's time to zoom in on the third: *answering the five questions every design needs.* I'll use my TV fast as a model and then follow with the final steps below (Appendix B contains simplified versions of the entire process).

Question 1: Purpose? You've named your issue and you've picked a design type. This question about purpose goes deeper.

After those months of watching countless hours of football, I knew I needed a prescriptive design. My illness required medication. That was the first and most obvious answer. More specifically, I needed to reset my relationship with the digital screen. I'm not a TV hater; the TV and I just needed to work out some issues. Simply unplugging it would not solve the problem. Finally, I needed space to see what was fueling my overconsumption. I didn't want to cut off the screen only to replace it with another unproductive habit.

> I'M NOT A TV HATER; THE TV AND I JUST NEEDED TO WORK OUT SOME ISSUES.

The more accurately I could name the reasons for pursuing a disruptive experience, the more success I would have in executing it. (Even diagnostic designs, which are open-ended by default, benefit from adding purpose-related details.)

Note that my reasons for designing an experience are specific to me. Your reasons may differ. In a conversation with author Al

Hsu, he said, "It may be appealing to go on a mission trip because of the intrigue of travel, or it could also be motivated out of evangelistic guilt or obligation. Someone may change their exercise habits because they're training for a marathon or because they had a heart attack scare."[3] Questions help unearth the why, clarifying motives by removing potential blind spots.

Question 2: Shape? Shape refers to the basic appearance and flavor of a design, regardless of type. For me, shape provided an answer for when friends asked, "So, Sam, what'd you decide to do about watching too much TV?"

"I decided to unplug it for Lent."

That's a fairly simple answer, but it's all about shape. What did my prescriptive experience look like? It looked like unplugging the television, and because it coincided with the season of Lent, it also looked like a spiritual fast. Those were two key shape elements. Think about it: I could have decided to keep the TV plugged in and address my problem instead with prayer alone or with an accountability partner I'd call if I watched more than two hours per week. Or I could have limited my TV viewing to documentaries or anything not about sports. Spiritual disciplines are meant to challenge us, and none of these options felt challenging to me. For that reason, shape mattered.

To take this example further, I might have chosen an altogether different shape and answered friends with "I decided to train for a marathon" or "I decided to use my Sunday afternoons to serve a disaster relief agency." Both would have occupied my time in useful ways, but I chose the shape I did because it had a fitting cost—that is, the shape complemented the purpose. I unplugged the TV because the TV was somehow my problem.

Question 3: Time? Fasting holds significant potential for growth. But how long should my fast from TV last? For me, a weekend was too short, and forever was too long. What began as a reaction to disgust now needed a levelheaded plan. Fasting the forty days of Lent felt right. I liked the symbolism of that length, since the number forty in the Bible nearly always pertains to a time of preparation or recovery. I also believed that this length of time would be long enough to suspend my "normal."

In the 1950s, Maxwell Maltz popularized the claim that it takes at least twenty-one days to form a habit. More recent research by Phillippa Lally shows sixty-six days to be the average.[4] Forty, I thought, was a fair enough split. In the end, because of new routines and healthier activities, it lasted close to 180 days!

In reference to time, I also needed to ask, When should it begin? I decided it should begin after the final play of the season. Lent would commence a week and a half later. Why not get a head start? That's the kind of immediacy I was looking for, and I loved the idea of fasting simultaneously with millions of Christians around the world. Solidarity equaled inspiration.

How often should it occur? I could have chosen to fast only on weekends or Sunday afternoons, but I wanted it to be full and continuous. On a related note, if I need a daily focus, how long should it be? Other than saying a short prayer every time my brain remembered, *Oh, hey, this is when you usually watch football*, I added nothing regimented. Interestingly, these short prayers faded as I replaced viewing time with new patterns. That isn't to say I stopped praying—just that these particular prayers lost their situational cues.

Would there be a time commitment for travel? No.

Would this fast require time from others to help me? Probably not.

Question 4: Cost? Cost pertains to an important set of questions, starting with this one: In what areas should (or would) this disruption cost me? I had several areas to consider beyond money, including physical, mental, relational, and spiritual. Here's how I answered them:

- *Financial.* Should there be a monetary cost? Not necessarily. But would there be, as a natural consequence? I figured the potential gain in productivity might lead to financial gain down the road. For example, using my weekends for home improvement projects instead of TV would increase the value of our house. (What actually happened was a mix of financial cost and gain. I had more time for those home improvements, but also more time for exercise and family activities, which led to buying items such as new shoes, games, and restaurant food.)

- *Physical.* No cost, only gain. Motion trumps loafing.

- *Mental.* I anticipated a combination of cost and gain here, too. I presumed cost might show up in the form of having to deal with whatever internal "noise" the TV had quieted, though I couldn't predict what this noise might be (stress? avoiding unpleasant chores? loneliness?). As for gain, I anticipated stimulation and a clearer conscience.

- *Social.* I assumed I'd have to say no to friends or family who might want to watch a movie, but I knew I'd gain in time spent together doing something else.

- *Spiritual.* If you want to call it a cost, I knew I'd have to trust the Lord to make this exercise worthwhile. And if I were able to hear whatever internal noise the TV had been quieting, would Jesus care enough to help me address it? It was only TV, but you know that a recurring headache can be symptomatic of anything from eyestrain to cancer. Perhaps that's too strong of an example, but it's true that we take a risk when we remove whatever numbs our pain, not only because we then have to feel that pain, but also because Jesus may decide not to remove it. Anesthetic habits, such as zoning out in front of a screen, hide that risk from sight.

Another cost question involves intensity: How far do I want to be pushed? I simply wanted a break. I wasn't looking for an activity that required a pep talk to start. I had no second thoughts. I never felt intimidated as I might on the eve of another kind of disruption, like tackling the entire Appalachian Trail. How far did I want to be pushed? Not far.

By the way, intensity can be applied to all five design questions. Also, there may be a sizeable difference between how far you *want* to be pushed and how far an experience *should* push you. For example, I took a group of out-of-shape twenty-somethings on a one-night backpacking trip because they wanted to grow in Christian maturity. They did not, however, want to climb a particularly long hill with full packs in the falling snow, despite signing up for it. And yet it was this stretch that gave one of the participants, Anna, what she needed. She said,

> I spent a lot of time watching where Marissa's feet were falling and telling myself that I couldn't slow down because I didn't want to separate her from the group or slow everyone down behind me. That made climbing that massive hill easier, because I was focusing on her and the group instead of myself and the hill ahead of us.

She added, "I feel like that's almost a metaphor." It is, indeed, Anna, and I'm thankful that you saw it. When there's a gap between *want* and *should*, it pays to lean toward the one that promises more growth.

Alternative ways to ask about cost include, What will I need to give up? and How much of my "normal" should be suspended?

Question 5: Location? Where should this experience take place?[5] My plan was the living room. Easy enough. But unplugging led to several other surprise locations, like the backyard and bike trails. Location can be a monastery, a train traveling across Europe, or a bungalow at the shore.

As is the case for all of these questions, there is overlap, which means location can relate to cost. When I turned twelve and Mom decided she had to get us away from Dad, she knew for her sake and for the sake of her four children that the location had to be sufficiently far away, so we moved to another state. This location decision had many costs, from financial to social, but the distance broke negative routines and established better ones for our family. Location matters.

SIGN UP!

At this point, you should have enough information to turn any design into an experience. You may need to attend to last-minute "packing," like scheduling time off work or getting someone to water your plants. There may be gear to purchase or money to raise. But it's time to send in your deposit. It's time to buy the tickets. It's time to get this thing on the calendar. Details make it real, but without a passport or a registration number, you've only got a plan. You've got to move the plan into action.

You've named your issue.

You've picked the type of experience you need.

You've filled in the details by answering at least the five questions above.

Now sign up!

Don't hesitate on this fourth step for fear of missing out on another opportunity or because you don't think you can do it. If you've made it this far, hesitations are likely due to perceived limitations, not actual limitations. That's an important distinction.

If you need to call a friend before you click Submit, do it. That friend will tell you the truth. The participation of others often encourages a design to take shape as well as helps us through the experience itself, so work through the details with a friend or mentor who will catch what you miss. Al Hsu notes, "Community is a factor—people go on trips because all their friends are going, or someone finally goes to AA after an intervention by concerned friends and family who invite them into the process."[6]

When Cat signed up for a mission trip to India, she couldn't predict what difference the community would make. At one difficult point, her trip leader offered assistance, but she said, "It's *my* burden. *I'm* doing this!" She asked God, "Why did you send me here? People are trying to take away my pride. What are you doing, God?" Reflecting on the trip afterward, she confessed, "I had this huge problem with pride and asking people for help . . . but I learned there that no matter what, God has your back and he's going to put people in your life that you can rely on and love, and be loved by."[7]

You received a prompt to grow. That's Jesus talking, and it would be a great loss to ignore him. Say yes. And say yes with a posture of receptivity—palms up and open to accept whatever might come.

Caution: A disruptive experience is not a savior. In fact, signing up does not guarantee intended results. So be patient and try again. Add to the cost or to the time. Change locations. And remember that Jesus may have an altogether different plan in mind for you.

BORROWING FROM OTHERS

Speaking of others, where does a design process like this come from? It belongs to me only as much as it belongs to XD and its director, Paul Harbison; to theorists and teachers like David Kolb, Parker Palmer, Jack Mezirow, and Ronald Heifetz; to Outward Bound founder Kurt Hahn before them; and to educational reformer John Dewey before him, and on back. The field of experiential education is filled with bright minds and faithful servants who have contributed decades of work for the sake of others. And our work today relies on that work—here a clear connection, there a synthesized philosophy.

This field began, in part, as a reaction to the Industrial Revolution, which, like its factory assembly lines, put children in classroom rows and promoted rote memorization and learning as a solely cognitive endeavor. Yet we are complex people. I learn from cutting myself on a saw blade and from reading a book, from falling in love and from trying to navigate the subway system in New York City.

John Dewey argued persuasively in the 1930s for an "organic connection between education and personal experience."[8] He criticized the traditional education system for attending only to the mind. In "A Christian Tin-Can Theory of the Human Person," philosopher Calvin Seerveld underscored the fact that we are more than simply physical and spiritual beings, but emotional, analytical, ethical, spatial, economic, political, aesthetic, and relational too.[9] We are like a tin can (a humble object, he says), whose ribs represent the varied and layered ways God's image is present in us.

One of my colleagues, Sean Purcell, has converted this idea into a group activity called Wheel of Person to help people appreciate their complexity. It's a simple series of questions, not much more than a get-to-know-you game in a sense, and yet it reveals unattended areas of our lives, which means a chance for learning.[10]

Limiting focus to a finite set of areas limits our potential growth. It also limits the potential for across-the-board health, as captured in this note on Seerveld's model: "An orthodox president without imagination or good social skills is not going to be a great asset, however orthodox he or she is. An orthodox pastor whose conservatism is tied into an undeveloped emotional life will cause havoc in a congregation."[11]

One way to avoid such blind spots is by reflecting, like Cat did in India. We might consider reflection a fifth step in the design process, after "Sign Up," though as we saw in the questions above, reflection happens throughout the process. I'll talk specifically about post-experience reflection in chapter seven, but here it is worth offering a few words about it as a way to credit those we borrow our ideas from.

According to transformative learning theorist Jack Mezirow, reflection matters. *Habits of mind* and *points of view*—our frames of reference—are deeply seated as "the result of cultural assimilation and the idiosyncratic influences of primary caregivers."[12] In other words, we don't think a lot about why we believe what we believe. Reflection uncovers how those frames of reference may be keeping us from maturing. The process involves (1) assessing assumptions, (2) becoming aware of our frames of reference and imagining different ones, and (3) dialoging with others.[13]

But who does this on a regular basis? Mezirow suggested that deep engagement typically follows a "disorienting dilemma"—a major disruption or crisis. For example, if I believe that all of my relationships are in perfect shape, it would be hard to see fault in them. I'd assume everything was fine. Coming to a different conclusion would require a disorienting dilemma, like betrayal, to alter my assumption.

Significant growth can be hard to come by, which is why *Disruptive Discipleship* aims at incremental, intentional jumps in maturity. It's not so much focused on making sense of a crisis, but on recognizing that we need to grow and that we need to create space for God to do that growing work.

This proactive approach reminds me of David Kolb's Experiential Learning Model (ELM), which has had a significant impact on outdoor education in particular because of the experiential aspect.[14] Below are its four components, with loose connections to my TV fast. Notice the important role reflection plays in this cyclical model:

- Concrete experience (feeling)—"I feel dissatisfied on Sundays."

- Reflective observation (watching)—"I've been sitting in front of the TV too much."

- Abstract conceptualization (thinking)—"I don't feel this way when I go for a run."

- Active experimentation (doing)—"I'm going to unplug the TV and go outside."

If the following Sunday produces more satisfaction (a new concrete experience), my new reflective observations should lead to new abstract conceptualizations and new active experimentations. By repeating the cycle over and over, without even thinking about it, I end up further each day from the dissatisfying experience of watching too much TV.

Like all theoretical tools, we borrow and build, adopt and adapt, remembering that they are meant to keep this simple message in focus: figure out what's holding you back, and do something about it.

Jesus loves doers. He loves couch potatoes too, but we're interested in people willing to work out their salvation. Zacchaeus gets the reward, not the rich young man; the widow's mite is esteemed, not the wealthy's spare change; the sinner's cry of "Lord, have mercy" reaches the throne, while the self-righteous declarations of the publican do not. It's the servant who invests the silver that reaps the reward while the treasure burier receives the lashing. Each time, the blessing goes to the one willing to do something about his or her situation—to the one willing to pay for it.[15]

If you're ready to pay for it, part two will show how to attach these concepts to the areas of faith, hope, and love.

DESIGN PRACTICE

Whether you spend six months or sixty seconds working through the design planning stages, the simple process I'm using is similar. Here's a little experiment to try as practice.

Step 1: Name the issue. You need a lumber cart at the Home Depot, but there are none inside because other customers left them in the parking lot. You have to go back outside to find one. This irritates you because you're losing valuable daylight for a Saturday project. After paying for and finally loading the materials in or on your vehicle, you hear yourself think, *I want to leave the cart out here as payback.*

Step 2: Determine what type of experience you should design. You know the issue: you're dealing with a spiteful attitude. So you know you can't leave the cart outside, even in a stall. Love is at stake here. Practicing the right thing will invite you to grow in it. You need a prescriptive design.

Step 3: Answer the five questions every design needs.

+ *Purpose?* To stop the revenge cycle.

+ *Shape?* Taking a cart into the store.

+ *Time?* Now.

+ *Cost?* Physically, a bit of uphill pushing; mentally, letting the bad guys win.

+ *Location?* Right here in the parking lot.

Step 4: Sign up. You have a plan. You need to implement it. So you walk the cart inside where it belongs.

In this experiment, getting to stage four takes less than a minute. There's no need to write anything down. You don't need to call a friend. Instead, you pray yourself back inside with a cart for the next shopper. It's likely that person will leave it in the parking lot again, but that isn't your concern.

Depending on personality, this kind of experience can be tough enough to learn from and easy enough to do in a snap. And practice like this provides confidence to take on bigger challenges down the road (like when it happens again tomorrow). Equally important, it familiarizes you with the process, a valuable step toward becoming a better designer and a more mature disciple.

Part Two

GROWING DEEPER

STEPPING OUT IN FAITH

4

Adventures in Trust

For the first two hundred feet or so past the entrance, daylight tumbles down into the corridor of boulders and forest debris. It makes the wet surfaces glisten. It's dark enough to switch on headlamps but light enough that we can't tell if they make a difference. Excitement and the stream below our feet make us raise our voices. We're going spelunking.

The first right turn in the cave is a thin crevice that moves us away from the water and light. The ten of us slip into it, shuffling and sidestepping over uneven stones, while the walls bump against us on both sides and occasionally pinch our helmets. I come to an intersecting passageway—one of hundreds in this underground labyrinth—and my left foot runs out of ground. I quickly shine my lamp in that direction and discover a five-foot drop. I had forgotten it was there. It wouldn't be a huge step for any of us, but we have to enter a hole on the other side in a crawling position. This will pose a challenge. I need to tell them what to do.

No one except for the person immediately behind me can see what I see. The space is simply too confined, and the other nine are attending to their own concerns anyway. It won't do much good instructing the entire group, so I explain the situation to the woman at my heels. Then I cross, and she inches forward, avoiding a potential fall now that she knows about the drop. She warns the caver immediately behind her. And so on. This is how we learn to trust the person in front of us and care for the one behind.

Forty-five minutes of hallways, cracks, holes, risk, and encouragement later, we arrive at a room large enough for all of us to make eye contact with each other. It's a relief to see everyone at once. We discuss the experience so far, drink water from our drag bags, adjust headlamps and helmets, and prepare for more difficult challenges ahead. Since that initial drop crossing, we haven't seen any outside light, though nobody realizes this yet. And we're far enough into the maze that few would find their way out without significant help.

It's difficult for me not to feel a sense of power. If I were to take their lights and disappear, the situation could become national news. But I'm a teacher, not a criminal, so I give a short lesson on the eastern pipistrelle bat.

We explore for hours, squeezing into smaller and smaller spaces like Keyhole, which requires us to exhale to pass through, and Birthing Canal, a seventy-foot-long, body-sized tube with one particularly frightening corner that can be traversed only by extending your arms in a diving position, lest you get stuck. But we also hop along streambeds and play on grand boulders. The group is gaining confidence.

Eventually we come to a large, sloped rock in the lower end of the cave. It's time for a test. They deposit their drag bags and follow me up a passageway—about thirty feet or so—to an intersection where I point back to the pile of gear. Their objective is to return to that location. The passage is tall enough to walk upright, and it's a straight shot, though uneven, and the walls come and go. To all observers, it appears to be a piece of cake.

Then I take their lights.

I walk quickly back to the slab and turn off mine too. They're on their own.

For the first time since the initial crevice, we can't see a thing. The air is blacker than night. Even after minutes of staring and squinting, the uneasy sense remains that our eyes have vanished. No sparkles on the calcite walls, no glimmer from headlamp lenses, no visible movements or shadows of any kind. Just pure, deep blackness.

The group members, alone and without visual aids, instinctively reach for each other. Those with navigational confidence offer suggestions. Caregivers ask questions. They collaborate for several minutes and appoint a leader. And then they begin what ought to be a five-second jaunt.

They use the communication method they've used all day: trusting and caring for the partners immediately in front and behind. Only now it matters more. Progress is slow, and by the second obstruction, they question not only their position and direction, but also the guide. All nine respond differently. Many have new ideas about where to go. A few become silent. Others joke to relieve the tension. After more time and more failed attempts, frustration increases. Fear creeps in.

I can hear them, of course. They're no closer or farther away than they were *twenty minutes* before, despite traveling short distances in every direction. As the sensation of being lost becomes real, they call out my name. They know I wouldn't desert them, but my silence and their tangible experience of disorientation—with friends they trust but who are also disoriented—unnerves them. They have absolutely no idea where they are.

After this painfully long time, I light a match. It illuminates the entire passage—not brightly, of course, but enough to alter the darkness so remarkably that everyone looks to it in relief.

In part one, we focused on going from being stuck to being ready. Discipleship is an active, continual process through which God, in his mercy, calls us "out of darkness into his wonderful light" (1 Peter 2:9). As we mature, we gain confidence to design more and sign up more. And we do so for the sake of growing in the big three: faith, hope, and love. This chapter focuses on faith.

COMFORT

We develop faith—a strong belief or trust in God—when we move, as Henri Nouwen wrote, "from false certainties to true uncertainties, from an easy support system to a risky surrender."[1] In other words, we grow by entering places where we've never been.

> GROWING IN FAITH REQUIRES THAT WE SUSPEND CONTROL, PAUSE SELF-RELIANCE, DISRUPT ROUTINE, AND SURRENDER OURSELVES TO THE UNKNOWN.

This movement involves numerous challenges. Growing in faith requires that we suspend control, pause self-reliance, disrupt routine, and surrender ourselves to the unknown. That's quite a formula for stress. Paul Johns, the marriage and family therapist from chapter one, explains, "The brain responds to stress by activating efficient self-protection mechanisms in order to avoid possible harm to self. This efficiency is good in some situations, particularly if a threat must be resisted quickly, but not good if efficiency reduces our ability to perceive more of the complexity and beauty of our world."[2] So this natural process can deter us from entering places we've never been—complex and beautiful places. This makes it challenging to grow in faith on purpose, since growing in faith requires uncertainty and risk (such as entering those stressful situations our brains want to avoid). Just ask the cavers.

Few would want everyday life to be so hard, even if it promised a double portion of faith.

False certainty, as Nouwen calls it, does this to us. It persuades us to believe that what we have now is not worth giving up to get the better thing we could have. Is growth *really* worth the hassle? Yet if we're convinced that maturity is worth pursuing and that faith leads to maturity and that moving toward risky surrender tests our faith, then despite our mental wiring, we must begin to practice letting go of the familiar. I, for one, dislike this notion more and more the older I get.

When we purchased our home, it took months of effort and sacrifice to fix it up. The work finally slowed enough for us to walk around town or swing on the porch as a family. I remember one evening when Julie asked, "How long do you think we'll live here?" I didn't hesitate: "Forever." Until this street address, I had moved over two dozen times. I was ready to settle down.

> **FALSE CERTAINTY PERSUADES US TO BELIEVE THAT WHAT WE HAVE NOW IS NOT WORTH GIVING UP TO GET THE BETTER THING WE COULD HAVE.**

Settle down. Something felt peaceful in that moment as I considered the prospect of staying put for a long time.[3] I could finally set up a woodworking shop. Our kids could attend the same school through graduation. We could plant a tree. The girls had been requesting a climbing tree for years, but it had never made sense. Now it did. Settling down encourages unpacking. It tells the pilgrim to set boots aside, say hello to the neighbors, get to know the street and the town it connects to, and consider how to serve the people who call it home.

Looking back, we see that God has blessed us in all of those ways. Even the tree we planted reminds us of abundance. "Forever" feels pretty good.

Then I recall Moses telling the Israelites, "When you eat and are satisfied, when you build fine houses and settle down, and when your herds and flocks grow large and your silver and gold increase and all you have is multiplied, then your heart will become proud and you will forget the LORD your God" (Deuteronomy 8:12-14).

I grew up listening to sermons about Israel's short-winded faith. I got it: God was remarkably good, and the people were unbelievably dull. God remembered; the people forgot. They whined and worried between flashes of praise, defaulting to faithlessness no matter what God did for them. This passage always conjured in my imagination a desperate crowd nodding eagerly at "build fine houses" while equally denying any possibility of "forget the LORD your God." But I knew their intentions wouldn't last. They don't last for me either.

We own 1,300 square feet of living space with a dirt basement below—not exactly the picture of prosperity by North American standards. But we enjoy enough elements of comfort to know what Moses meant. I predicted in 2010 when Julie asked, "How long?" that comfort would come. It is simply what happens when routine sets in. A measly three hundred square feet, let alone thirteen hundred, can make us forget God, given enough time and routine.

Settling down is not evil, and building a fine house may be wise. But when we pursue a still *finer* house and a *softer* bed and a bike with springs in the seat and an emergency fund to back up our emergency fund, and we insure the whole lot with premiums that siphon money automatically from bank accounts that are also insured, and we do it without any reminders of how prone we are to forget, then we will forget.

Here's the thing about false certainty: it offers the sensation of control without actually giving it to us. It offers confidence to the cavers until the light goes out and they realize their helplessness. It offers comfort to homeowners until rates go up or pay goes down, and they face their inability to rescue themselves. People with false certainty don't need God, because we don't believe we face any real risks. It's the unawareness of these risks that pauses our faith.

CHAOS

There is a flipside to the absence of risk, you know: too much risk. If settling down threatens to stagnate our faith, speeding up threatens to overextend it. Neither fosters maturity, because both say to God, "I don't care." The settler does nothing to bring his faith to life. The fire breather can't seem to refrain from toying with death.

My friend Todd owned a Ford Mustang that had been upgraded with numerous racing components, and the turbo gauge and aftermarket tachometer on the dash told us what those components were doing. I had experienced a few fast cars before, but when we broke a hundred miles per hour by the end of an uphill freeway entrance ramp, and my head and frame and lungs were pressed hard against the seat, all laughter and idle talk ceased. My face flushed. Traffic and vision blurred, and there in the midst of the deafening roar came a deadly silence.

Those brief seconds offered no place for thoughts on legacy or whether I had made amends with a sibling; they made no room to question whether Todd and I would get heaven or hell for this, though the intensity of the moment made each of them seem appropriate. The only squeezed-out prayer begged that nothing would jump from the berm into our jet path.

That much power in such a proximate way amazed me. What caused my adrenaline to climax also scared me. I knew even then, in my early twenties, that that kind of experience in that particular place at that hour of the night could be replicated only so many times before ending poorly.

So I amended my ways by switching to other thrills: hauling friends behind the car on a sled, jumping from a moving train, rappelling from the center of a seven-hundred-foot-long railroad bridge between speeding train runs, rappelling from a highway overpass in the dark, clearing fifty miles per hour on a residential street on a mountain bike. What was I thinking? This combination of thrill seeking, inexperience, and lack of judgment is exactly why auto premiums are so high for young (male) drivers. We think we're invincible, still wearing Incredible Hulk Underoos on a quest to find that magical place where human limits touch superhuman potential.

This is chaos because it's out of order. When I overextend my faith by acting with poor judgment, I scramble the way things were meant to be. And God is not a ripcord to be pulled whenever I decide to pull it.

JUST RIGHT

Somewhere between comfort and chaos is the sweet spot where maturity can flourish. Harvard Professor Ronald Heifetz calls this the Productive Zone of Disequilibrium. "It is like a pressure cooker: set the temperature and pressure too low, and you stand no chance of transforming the ingredients in the cooker into a good meal. Set the temperature and pressure too high, and the cover will blow off the cooker's top, releasing the ingredients of your meal across the room."[4]

HEROISM

There are times, however, when we may need to overextend our faith. In the animated movie *Big Hero 6*, Hiro and his robot sidekick, Baymax, pass through an unstable portal to save the enemy's daughter. They are not adrenaline junkies in this moment, but heroes, and though survival is unlikely, they go. In the Marvel superhero movie *The Avengers*, enemy drones threaten the planet until Iron Man steers a nuclear missile toward the mothership responsible for hatching the swarm. Through a portal in the heavens, he flies to save humanity and surely to die. It is his most selfless act.

Pop culture examples like these highlight a certain kind of faith. Rey in *Star Wars: The Force Awakens*, Pai in *Whale Rider*, Dr. Neville in *I Am Legend*. We are captivated by their stories, not because they represent comfort and not because of the adrenaline rush, but because they are heroes who act for the sake of others. Despite the gross improbability of success, we want to be heroes too.

Interestingly, in the moments before heroes enter chaos, they go through the design stages we discussed in chapter three: they perceive an issue, select a design to address it and fill in a few details, and then sign up. They may have only four seconds to do it, but they do it. This leaves little time to process risk, but unlike the junkie, they put their life on the line for service, not pleasure. The one pulls people out of the fire; the other simply plays with it. Even an adrenaline junkie like Iron Man's Tony Stark—who taunts mortality with flying suits—occasionally manages to surrender his inflated ego.

Few of us face portals unless we are law enforcement officers, first responders, or the like. It doesn't take away from the fact that we're drawn to enter them. This good kind of adrenaline comes in handy when unwelcomed experiences strike those around us.

Like comfort, though, heroism still tempts us to put too much faith in ourselves. We love what the Hollywood stars do, because their actions address human potential. But Jesus' act of passing through the portal of the cross addresses human *limitation*. Iron Man implies, "You can do it with the right technology and the right friends and the right timing," to which Jesus responds, "I want you to know something about yourself: Iron Man is on a movie set." Despite the difficult feats Jesus tells us to perform, and the promise he makes that we'll do even more than he did, he proves that his greatest act is impossible to replicate. We are more likely to don a bulletproof super suit, fly into an actual extraterrestrial dimension, and destroy a giant alien war-beast singlehandedly. Jesus' heroism saves us, and every time we fall in the slightest way, it reminds us that we can't save ourselves.

Moving from false certainty to true uncertainty means paying attention to the balance between comfort and chaos, between the absence and abundance of risk. It calls for a grounded approach that involves (1) knowing ourselves, (2) recognizing God at work, and (3) being prepared for a dangerous period following the signup, called the middle ground.

FAITH MOVEMENT

Knowing ourselves. When I turned forty, a series of challenges disrupted what I knew about myself. Insecurity mounted as peers acquired degrees I didn't have and built businesses I wouldn't know how to run. Comparing myself to them corrupted an already faulty ranking system. Fantasies I had held for decades proved to be fruitless. In one arena after another, I encountered inability. I wasn't the superhero I imagined I would become.

At first, and for quite some time, these humbling realizations sucked the wind out of me. Down I went, questioning what I had contributed to the world and wondering what could possibly be done to remedy my lack. Anybody who has been there knows it can be a dark place.

Eventually, a shift occurred. Those humbling realizations morphed into points of confession. I had to surrender my fantasies regarding future prospects and vision, since most of that future was not mine to dream—like getting into the NFL at six three and 170 pounds. With each release, I discovered more freedom. I was simultaneously coming to the end of myself and finding a new space to inhabit. I didn't want to settle for comfort by cutting off my aspirations. Nor did I want to keep feeding the adrenaline junkie to simulate a reality that wasn't mine. And if I happened to be a hero at some point along the way, so be it; but I needed to leave that up to God.

Knowledge improves compatibility between who we are and what we need in order to mature. A prescriptive experience designed to help me through that particular patch involved making a list of careers and skills I had fantasized about for years, then letting them go one at a time. But I couldn't do it until I recognized my immaturity and came to terms with who God created me to be.

Knowledge also gives us a sense of what would stretch us and what would not. If you were asked to rappel down a rock face tomorrow, you would quickly think of reasons for or against it. If you are acrophobic, the heights would cripple you. If you are clumsy, you'd choose flatter ground. If you trust the guide, you'd feel safe. If you understand biophysics, equipment usage, and technique, you'd believe you could lead the experience. I have friends who know enough that while they appear to be taking great risks, they're actually playing it safe, even as their feet dangle over a canyon. For them, it isn't chaos or comfort, but balance—a healthy display of faith.

The challenge is knowing whether what we know about ourselves should be pushed or held back. Fear can shortchange the truth, keeping us from taking necessary risks because they feel bigger than they really are. Arrogance has the opposite effect. And our community can often see what balance would look like in us better than we can.

So whether you are forty or eighteen, take an inventory of your fantasies in order to develop a realistic faith. Address your fear of heights to help you grow in relying on Jesus. If you have more years under your belt, take a sabbatical and learn how the office can manage without you. Serve the poor to discover your own poverty, or trust your kids to try something without you holding their hands. Turn out the light, and realize how lost in the dark you are without it.

Recognizing God. Knowing ourselves is a critical step toward maturing in faith. It shows us what great things we can do and connects us to the reality of our limitations. These same observations teach us to recognize God's role in our lives. The great things elicit praise for his handiwork, and the limitations cause us to seek his help. Of course, if I take things for granted, I'm liable to miss both of these.

Recognition requires attentiveness. When I notice that my car starts—when I actually realize that it didn't *not* start—I have an opportunity to show gratitude for a car that starts. So I do. I say, "Thank you, Lord, for a car that starts." It's an elementary exercise and yet a powerful one, in part because attentiveness, which leads to recognition, has access to memory. The moment I offer this little prayer, I realize that the prayer was true yesterday, too, and a hundred mornings before that.

GRATITUDE CUTS THROUGH THE NUMBING ELEMENTS OF ROUTINE. Gratitude cuts through the numbing elements of routine. It makes us mindful of those things that we take for granted, like starting a car. At my first teaching job out of college, I'd pass the high school janitor and ask, "How are you today, Gerome?"

And every day, with genuine gratitude, he'd respond, "Sam, I'm able to sit up and take nourishment."

By acknowledging the existence of the basics—whatever those may be for each of us—we build faith by recognizing faithfulness.

> As the rain and the snow
>   come down from heaven,
> and do not return to it
>   without watering the earth
> and making it bud and flourish,
>   so that it yields seed for the sower and bread for the eater,
> so is my word that goes out from my mouth:
>   It will not return to me empty. (Isaiah 55:10-11)

This access to memory works in a forward direction as well. Because God was faithful yesterday, my faith is bolstered for tomorrow. History is a great informant. It contains the small details that reveal God's character as well as the sweeping narratives that reveal his activity. Why would I think that this faithful activity will suddenly cease?

Faithfulness tomorrow may not look the same as it did yesterday. The car may not start, but a neighbor sees my plight and offers a ride to work. Or my boss gives me a project to work on at home instead. Regardless of what pans out, paying attention gives rise to recognition of how God provides, which expands my breadth of expectation for his faithfulness in the future. Who knows how the Lord will show up, but he will, and I begin to look forward to how.

All of this reveals an important truth: *I am capable of demonstrating faith.* If I worried every time I got in the driver's seat, imagine how paralyzing it would be. Perhaps this is you. Anxiety does strange things to us. In a vehicle with frequent problems, it makes sense that some worry appears with the turning of the key, but not under normal conditions. Otherwise, how could we plan ahead? How could we promise to pick up a friend or go on a trip?

If you think you are paralyzed, I don't think you are. You're reading a book, which is like turning that key. Recognize God's work even in such small acts, and give thanks.

There is a second truth: *I am capable of growing in faith.* As a professional fisherman, the disciple Peter *demonstrated* faith (casting nets into the dark for a living is either a foolish gamble or an investment based on historical outcomes). He was also capable of *growing* in faith, despite it coming in fits and starts. When he accepted the invitation to be a disciple, he watched Jesus perform miracles like feeding thousands of people without a grocery store in sight. Then he tried walking to Jesus on the water and fell in fear. "Immediately Jesus reached out his hand and caught him. 'You of little faith,' he said, 'why did you doubt?'" (Matthew 14:31).

Was Peter actually a man "of little faith"? Or was he rushing into big acts of faith before the little acts had settled into place? Maybe Peter hadn't watched enough yet. I admire the risk he took, though. He got out of the boat because he recognized who was calling him. Eventually, Peter would trust so deeply that he would give his life for Jesus. That's growth.

So how do we grow in faith, practically speaking? We keep paying attention. We get to know ourselves. We recognize and acknowledge God at work. We keep showing up in challenging places—in the cave, on a justice mission, at the door of a friend who could make better decisions but doesn't and so he needs our help again. There, in the challenge, our senses are more fine-tuned to the great things the Lord has enabled us to do as well as to the limitations that cause us to turn to him. We show up like Peter showed up, over and over, until we get it, giving thanks for whatever happens in the process. All the while, we must be prepared for that space between stepping out in faith and realizing that stepping out was worth it.

Preparing for the middle ground. This move from, as Nouwen said, "an easy support system to a risky surrender" usually takes time. We plan with a specific end in mind, and though an intense experience may produce a sudden aha moment, we can't guarantee the outcome. Growth likes open spaces. Instead of saying, "This service experience on this day will renew my faith in this unique way," we say, "Jesus, I'm signing up to serve, but I don't really want to. Will you help me see why this is important and where I need to grow?" After all, if criteria could produce exactly what we desire, why would we need faith?

Because movement takes time, it implies the existence of a space in-between. Let's say I decide in March to run a marathon in October. I'm registering today for a daunting task that is seven months away. That is an act of faith. And there are seven months of interruptions, soreness, hard work, and temptation to talk me out of it. This until-then period is the middle ground, the dangerous time between commitment and completion, between signup and execution.

In Mitch's youth ministry, he invites teens to walk away from the trouble they're in by introducing them to Jesus. He wants to replace their illusions with truth. Shayna is hungry for attention. A boy and a certain crowd want to provide it for her. Drama rules at home, and Shayna will do anything to quiet all the noise. She has no real sense of consequences from the poor decisions being offered, and she can hardly remember (let alone comprehend) what was said when her grandmother dragged her to church last month. For some reason, though, Shayna holds off long enough to text Mitch, and she gets a response that makes sense—even convincing her of a better way. As frail and rebellious as she feels, she commits to it.

What a good-news story! Shayna turns from death to life, from false certainty to true—oh, and there it is: *uncertainty*. The middle ground. She's enamored by a vision of the future, but like Peter in the courtyard at Jesus' trial, she still has to get there, and tomorrow morning on the bus will be the first test to see what her commitment is really made of. Does she know herself—whether she's the type who needs minor encouragement or perhaps a new school altogether? Can she recognize God's presence and provision when old haunts, impatience, and exhaustion threaten to dismiss it? Is Shayna aware of just how incapable she is of self-sustainability and, ultimately, self-rescue?

Knowing ourselves—what tempts us, what motivates us—helps to define our relationship with our faith: Is it too soft? Is it too reckless? Where does it need to be challenged? There is often a lot of ground to cover between what that knowledge reveals and what it requires.

Learning to recognize God in difficult spaces enables us to navigate that ground (more on this in chapter seven). This recognition also develops in us the perseverance to press on. For Sara, one of my caving participants, being able to see like this was huge. "I remember trusting you as a leader," she said, "which helped me relax into the adventure. There were moments that were really narrow and scary, but we made it! Isn't that how it feels with God leading?" Yes, especially when we can see him at work.

But what about when we can't see? Eve describes it like this: "There was something very visceral about the cave experience. It had to do with receiving continual sensory input from my hands and feet, which gave me a heightened sense of body awareness." Eve is an occupational therapist now, which influences her translation of what happened. "I felt fully grounded in there. But the trust walk in the dark, that was different. I became way more skeptical of my safety and surroundings, and it pointed out to me that I really only trusted what I could see and feel. It was hard to believe in just a voice. That was a contrast that has stuck with me." When all we have is a voice—or harder yet, when there is no voice but "just a promise" (as Eve went on to say)—we discover what our faith is made of.

The task, then, is to find balance between too much comfort and too much chaos, and that is where designed experiences can open a whole new realm of faith.

DO IT: DESIGNS TO GROW IN FAITH

Actions that develop faith happen because, like prayer, they move us "from false certainties to true uncertainties, from an easy support system to a risky surrender," as Henri Nouwen said. Surrendering control is risky indeed. Here are a few sample designs ranging from minor to major. Keep in mind that anyone can enter challenges like these and grow from them. Yet we aren't interested primarily in personal growth, but growth in the belief that God *can*. Our aim is maturing as disciples of Christ.

Go caving. Why not? If the thought scares you, start touristy where the paths are lit and lined to keep you safe and there's a gift shop at the end. Want to lengthen your stay and still not get dirty? Check out the Beckham Creek Cave Lodge in the Ozarks of Arkansas, an exclusive treat running a mere $1,600 per night (beckhamcave.com)! For a lot more dirt and a lot less money, take a wild cave tour with the Georgia Girl Guides (georgiagirlguides.com).

Connection: "Do I believe God can lead me through unfamiliar places when all I have is a voice or a promise?"

Let go of one fantasy. Remember my NFL dream? Yeah, say goodbye to craziness. You are more than you think, but let's be reasonable.

Connection: "Do I believe God can provide worth for me?"

Do one thing you're afraid of. Ride a bigger roller coaster, leave your hand sanitizer at home, ask for a raise, tell your friend to stop. "Baby steps," Bob Wiley would say in the movie *What About Bob?* And look where he ended up.

Connection: "Do I believe God can meet me in my fear?"

Test your generosity. Tithe a full 10 percent of your income, even if you're struggling to make ends meet. That struggle is often perceived more than actual. According to research by the Barna Group, "It's not just how much Americans actually make that impacts their giving—it's also how they feel about how much they make."[5] Barna Group president David Kinnaman notes that "evangelical Christians seem to be the most content financially (regardless of household income); they are more likely to feel they have more money than they need, and less likely to feel they are struggling." Is this related to faith? Regardless, an increase in generosity has real-world implications.[6]

You can also test your generosity by buying two of everything for a month and giving the second away. Or pay for the groceries directly behind you, no matter how full your neighbor's cart happens to be.

Connection: "Do I believe God can provide?"

REDISCOVERING HOPE

5

Tests of Endurance

In an article called "Couples Camping," Rachel Zurer wrote about the effect of unexpected snow during a trip in Wyoming's Wind River Mountains:

> We trudge along our off-trail route at less than a mile per hour, flakes still falling. Above treeline, a short section of boulder-hopping becomes a minefield of slippery rocks and ankle traps. We can hardly see the pass we're supposed to climb. "Let's just stop here for tonight," I finally suggest.
>
> It's an awful campsite, exposed to the raging winds, but turning back seems worse than enduring it. Danny's feet have turned white and icy in his soaking-wet boots; I press them against my stomach for as long as I can bear. Every minute or two a gust sends the walls of our tent tilting in one direction or another. We brace ourselves to hold the shelter steady, neither of us willing to ponder what might happen if the poles snap. Sometime in the middle of the long, long night, I start crying, and he kisses the wetness off my cheeks.

By the time the sun finally burns off the clouds, we don't just *think* we can get through hard times together. We *know* it.[1]

Ah, young love. It looks with tremendous optimism at an unknown future. And with nary a few days of hardship under its belt, it believes it has been fired in the smelting furnace of permanence. And yet I believe Rachel is speaking the truth. Will she and Danny last through a miscarriage or two, skin cancer, addictions, or whatever other threat that can move into a marriage over time? I don't know, but I certainly want them to. One thing they've got going for them: in the years since that tough night, they've continued to camp together. A practice like that contributes to the ability to persevere.

Hope is the "feeling of expectation and desire for a particular thing to happen," according to the Oxford Dictionary. Rachel may have entered their relationship merely hoping they could get through hard times. But now that they had actually made it through some hard times, that hope was turning into faith. That's right: hope converting to faith. She said as much: "We don't just *think* we can get through hard times together. We *know* it." That's a faith statement because, in a general way, it's based on "the assurance of things hoped for, the conviction of things not seen" (Hebrews 11:1 ESV). How can we hope for something we don't believe can happen?

I once promised students in Pennsylvania a great week of backpacking in Utah. To create faith for their hope to feed on, I interrupted three days of driving with random activities like sled riding on the side of the highway and pulling a man's car from the ditch. By the time we arrived at the trailhead—two thousand miles across the country—memories caused the students to believe it would indeed be a great week of backpacking. My design helped them form a "conviction of things not seen."

Rachel and Danny have something going for them because every time they sign up for another experience, they create another morsel of faith for their hope to feed on. With each rain-soaked, wind-pressed, snow-numbed, ice-covered success, the belief that they *can* make it strengthens the hope that they *will* make it. These mini-tests improve their expectations, Oxford says, "for a certain thing to happen," making the next test less of a threat to the future of their marriage. Does this make sense? Proof that I made it today causes me to believe I will make it tomorrow, even if the details are different.

But hope is more than this. For as much as I like Zurer's commitment and Zamperini's resilience, hope extends beyond inspirational tales of self-reliance, because hope—in the noun form, if you will—exists outside of ourselves. According to Hebrews 6:19, it's an anchor, and anchors attach to immovable objects and to forces larger than us. If I could muster hope on my own, what need would I have for supernatural provision? If I relegate hope to fallible constructs, like marriage or succeeding at a quest, what will sustain me when I inevitably run out of myself?

In the two seasons I've watched the TV show *Alone*, most contestants, regardless of the presence or absence of religious beliefs, eventually turn to God. These are people who signed up to suffer by spending as many as sixty-five days in a punishing environment with minimal gear and no communication with the world.[2]

For one contestant, Larry, it happened when he could no longer bear the monotony and lack of calories on Vancouver Island. For Jose, it happened when much-needed supplies appeared miraculously on shore. For David, it was when he couldn't take the separation from family anymore. When their own skills couldn't provide, when personal mental stamina failed to keep them sane, they turned beyond themselves. (Spoiler alert: interestingly, the winners of both seasons included one who regularly recited Bible verses for strength and one who had been a pastor.)

There is a reason we seek the Almighty in desperate moments: we are dependent creatures. At some point, like all of us, Rachel and Danny will their limits with each other and require more than personal fortitude. Where will they turn then?

The apostle Paul knew something about hope as a beyond-the-self concept. Here is a guy who suffered flogging, stoning, incarceration, sleeplessness, threats, nakedness, and exposure to death, and still wrote in Romans 12:12, "Be joyful in hope." (This pain-filled list from 2 Corinthians 11:23-29 was written *before* his optimistic declaration in Romans 12.) How? Because having witnessed God's faithfulness time and again, he found a place to attach the anchor of hope. Confirmation of completed things directly impacted his expectation of coming things, and when pushed beyond his capacity, he came to see the Lord as a firm foundation, external and immovable.

HOPE IN OUR RELATIONSHIPS WITH EACH OTHER MUST BECOME HOPE IN THE CREATOR OF THOSE RELATIONSHIPS.

Through this promise-fulfillment cycle, Paul discovered the confidence that comes at the close of suffering. There he found joy—not dread, not fatalistic ruminations, not woe-is-me pessimism about his rough life, but joy that comes from seeing God's character and actions over time.

Is Paul's experience all that different from Rachel's and Danny's? Not entirely. Both suffered. The suffering might have felt similar in the moment. But it's important to note the one-step-further part of the process. Hope in our relationships with each other must become hope in the Creator of those relationships. Enduring hardship by hoping our strength lasts must become hope in the One who gives that strength. I don't want to simply Christianize a concept here. There is a real difference between wishful thinking and confidence, between knocking on wood and stepping out in a certainty that exceeds our probability of success in this present moment of suffering. And we don't gain this certainty overnight.

Again, what's the point of hardship if it results only in self-confidence? There is a big point. For all of us—both the Rachels and the Pauls—designed experiences push us to remember that we are unable to make it on our own. The choice, then, especially at the point of breaking, is in what—in Who—we place our hope.

HOLDING ON

In the northern half of the Dolly Sods Wilderness, West Virginia, extensive logging and fires in the late 1800s and early 1900s left behind a barren landscape. Various accounts state that between two and nine feet of humus soil were destroyed, and because this plain sits atop a mountain plateau, it became completely exposed to the weather. The result is an ecology resembling parts of northern Canada.

Over the past one hundred years under federal protection, the flora in this section has tried to come back. Similar to plants that sprout from volcano ash, flora has returned, but not without challenges. In the places where the humus burned down to the rock, shallow soil can support only grasses and hard, low-growing shrubs. Trees here are generally stunted and sporadic, struggling in clumps with little to no shelter from the harsh winds.

On any given late-summer afternoon in this tough place, it isn't uncommon to see sunshine, hail, rain, and snow in back-to-back intervals. One minute, you're hiking in sunglasses and a T-shirt; the next, you're wrapped in winter gear and seeking shelter from the squall. (Just this week we were planning a quick visit to Dolly Sods, and the forecast for Sunday is snow, with gusts of over forty miles per hour, a wind-chill of ten degrees, and periods of sun—on April 3.)

Within the lineup of weathered characters is my favorite: the flag-form spruce. For the most part, this tree is a regular old red spruce, *Picea rubens*, an evergreen native to northeastern United States capable of reaching eighty feet. But the term "flag-form" or "flagged" makes it something special. Struggling to reach twenty feet, these exposed specimens look worn and thin, their sparse branches a haggard weave of needles and bare twigs, oddly growing on only one side. This is how they got their name.

The western side of the trunk may be nearly, if not completely, branchless, except for an occasional woody projection. Looking at them from the north, you see struggling branches on the left and nothing on the right, kind of like a flag. Some appear to be so far gone that you'd think they were dead, just dry remains of torture.

Now for the good part. One of the most inspirational examples lives among Bear Rocks, a massive strip of boulders along the edge of the Dolly Sods plateau. This tree has nothing to protect it from the elements that pass through its remaining branches. It is roughly eighteen feet tall and is, as I've described, branchless on the right and haggard on the left. The few branches on its "good" side are narrow and see-through—until you reach the bottom, that is. For at the bottom there is one branch, the lowest branch, which shoots outward toward the east for *eighteen* feet. That's the same length as the tree is tall. But it is three feet thick and fifteen feet wide, with long, full, green needles on every surface. It wraps around and over the stones and hides itself among the knee-high forest of bushes that live at Dolly Sods. Those bushes include blueberry and huckleberry, and lower plants like wintergreen and raspberry, all nestled in and forming a packed pantry for animals and people that feed on its delights.

~18 feet

My favorite flag-form specimen of *Picea rubens* at Bear Rocks, Dolly Sods Wilderness, West Virginia. The measurement shows the length of the bottom branch, which is nearly as long as the tree is tall. *(Photo by Sam Van Eman)*

It's a miraculous thing, really, and every time I see it, I'm again surprised by how it works. Like its companions, this tree has learned to endure. It doesn't have a cruise-control life. Every day brings the possibility of challenge, and every day, as it loses a few more needles up top or another branch snaps off and blows over the edge into the valley below, that one branch on the ground extends farther, like a photosynthetic solar panel. If the branches could talk to each other, they would say, like Rachel, "We don't just *think* we can get through hard times together. We *know* it."

Personally, I don't want to live in a brutal environment or be exposed to constant punishment, however helpful it may be. I don't want to be flogged. In eighth grade, I was accused of fighting in the hall and was sent to the dean, who paddled me so hard my feet came off the carpet. Let me tell you, it's no fun. I don't want to be stoned or shipwrecked or naked with no food. And yet I want to mature. So I sign up for experiences that mimic their lessons to some degree. If I go to Dolly Sods, it isn't to live there year-round; it isn't to become that flag-form spruce. (I'm still too immature to sign up for such bravery.) Rather, it's to show up for a few days of hiking to see what I'm made of and to be tested a little more than I am in my normal daily routine. *Bicycling* magazine put it this way: "Some do the ride even though they can't do the ride, and eventually they can do the ride. Some never do the ride, and can never do the ride."[3]

This is why we pursue challenges. They train us to expect differently. Hope relies on a memory bank of faith confirmations, increasing our patience and teaching us to adapt when comfort gets postponed or when life as we planned it

> EXPECTANCY—CHARACTERIZED BY ADAPTABILITY, NOT PREDICTABILITY— CREATES SPACE FOR GOD TO WORK.

suffers alterations. Challenges reveal a home where the anchor of our hope can rest. Expectancy—characterized by adaptability, not predictability—creates space for God to work.

COUNTING TO FIVE-MISSISSIPPI

In a blog entry, Shawn Smucker confessed:

> There are many things I would wish into my present, if I could: a little more money, a few more projects, kids that sleep through the night and don't end up on your floor at various nope-o'clock hours. A box of Lucky Charms and a gallon of whole milk all to myself. The temptation for me while waiting, with my personality and background and temperament, is to make drastic changes, either in an attempt to rush things or to so drastically change the game itself that what I was waiting for no longer applies. We'll move! I'll get a job! I'll sleep all day! I'd rather blow up this beautiful life I'm living than sit around and wait.[4]

Shawn's reflection (he made none of those irrational moves, by the way) brought to mind a conversation I had with a group of college students about the importance of trusting God through hard times. We were looking at Psalm 84:5-7:

> Blessed are those whose strength is in you,
>> whose hearts are set on pilgrimage.
> As they pass through the Valley of Baka,
>> they make it a place of springs;
>> the autumn rains also cover it with pools.
> They go from strength to strength,
>> till each appears before God in Zion.

It's an example of hope in action. These were people who chose movement over comfort, and difficulty over ease (*Baka* sounds like the word for "weeping" or "tears" in Hebrew). And like the flag-form spruce, they were finding strength along the way.

A colleague jumped into the discussion with a reading from William Bridge's sermon "Saints Should Not Be Discouraged Whatever Their Condition Be":

> Know ye, therefore, any man that is in this valley of Baca, where no water is, yet if he can find in his heart to dig up pits, to pray, read, hear, meditate, confer, and perform duties; though those duties be empty of comfort for the present, yet the rain of grace and mercy shall fall upon those pits, and he shall go from strength to strength until he appear before the Lord in glory.[5]

This is how we do it. We dig because we cannot provide for ourselves, or because we need to learn that we are incapable of self-sustainability. Whatever the reason, we dig and then wait for the rain to come.

Patience teaches us to favor the unknown. It is a sign of believing that the rain *will* come, and even if it doesn't (Daniel 3:16-18), we can't turn to another source. In this way, we learn to appreciate

God's surprises. We go, God provides, faith increases, and hope feeds on it. We go a little further, God provides again, and the cycle continues. And we mature because that's the effect the cycle has. Each little test and every minute of waiting for a need to be met delivers another strength and teaches us to whine less as we lack less (James 1:4). Hope feeds on faith.

The temptation, of course, is to give up. King David closed Psalm 27 by saying, "Wait for the LORD; be strong and take heart and wait for the LORD" (v. 14). Here he is all hope, with the patient-waiting kind of hope that looks past current struggles until the day when the Deliverer comes. But that's the *last* line of the Psalm. The *first* line says, "The LORD is my light and my salvation—whom shall I fear? The LORD is the stronghold of my life—of whom shall I be afraid?" And I ask, *What if David were to become afraid between verse 1 and verse 14, between where he begins and where he ends, in that middle ground between the declaration of faith and the realization of hope?*

What if the enemy David has in mind in verse 1 turns out to be bigger than he imagined, so that he gives up on God before getting to verse 14? He'll either surrender to the enemy threatening his safety—a true confession that God is *not* a stronghold—or he'll take matters into his own hands—a true confession that David himself is a *better* stronghold. Both sever the connection between faith and hope. Faith says God can; hope says God will. And this makes me wonder, *Is it too simplistic to say that if I don't wait, then I don't believe?*

CHRONIC ADAPTATION

Chronic adaptation is "the way your body meets the challenge of cumulative exercise, i.e., getting stronger and more beast-like."[6]

How does an inspirational quote like this one affect our belief that God is a better stronghold?

Last summer, my daughters asked me to time how long they could hold their breath underwater. We had a hotel pool to ourselves, and I told them to start when ready. The first time, they both popped up around twenty-five seconds, huffing and puffing. They thought they could do slightly better, and so did I, so down again they went. This time they passed thirty. They smiled at the improvement, but the third and fourth rounds remained about the same. They had maxed out, it seemed. I asked if I could offer a piece of advice (I usually volunteer it, but I didn't want to spoil their fun). They said yes.

"Try taking deep, slow breaths before you start. It will help open your lungs." This got them into the forties.

"What else can we do, Dad?" they asked now with anticipation. I had ideas. (I was also, ironically, planning to give a talk on hope the next day. Why not do a little experiment with my girls?) "This time, play dead in the water. Don't move a muscle. And if you have to come up for air before your sister does, keep the water still for her. Calm is key." They took their breaths, inhaled fully, and relaxed into the water.

Forty-five seconds later, Alice, my youngest, popped up, with Emma about ten seconds after that. Both had new records. Both were also declaring to each other that they couldn't possibly stay under any longer. They feared they had reached their limits.

"That's crazy talk," I interrupted. "Of course you can. You've already more than doubled your time since the first round. I'm confident you can reach a minute, and I have a new trick to help you get there." They looked at me with big eyes. Alice—the idealist—agreed to the challenge and started getting ready. Emma told her to wait. "Dad hasn't given us the new trick yet." As a planner, she knew she'd need more help.

"Okay," I said, leaning forward in my chair. "Do you know that point when you're holding your breath and it gets so hard that your stomach tightens and your eyes want to pop and you feel like you're going to burst if you don't breathe?"

"Yes! That's when we come up for air," they chimed in.

"Well, don't. Right then, when all you want to do is quit, count to five-Mississippi and *then* come up. Got it?"

"We'll try."

Something happened that I didn't expect. They both made it (that much I predicted), but Emma surpassed her record by twenty seconds. "How did you do it?" I asked. This is what she said: "I did like you told us and counted to five at the end, but when I got to five, I realized I could probably count to five again. So I did, and then I did it again and then one more time until I was really, really out of breath."

The experiment worked. Earlier, the girls had been testing their abilities on their own with very little success or progress. Then a few factors came into play:

- They invited outside assistance. This created accountability by way of external incentive.

- They asked to be timed, which introduced self-competition and performance.

- They welcomed advice, showing teachability and the opportunity to gain technique.

- They responded to clear goals. By setting targets, they knew how far they had to go. (In a later round, for example, I tapped on their shoulders every thirty seconds to help with pace.)

- They pushed themselves into new territory, which proved they were capable of more.

We continued for several more rounds until each of them stopped progressing, only seconds from the two-minute mark. *Two minutes*, up from twenty-five seconds. Whether they could have done more, it's hard to say. There are limits, after all, as well as the need to exercise discernment. But it was clear that pushing and being pushed led to new faith moments that hope could feed on.

We all have those moments when we're desperate for air or for deliverance from the enemy or just for our own box of Lucky Charms. This is when we count to five-Mississippi.

"I WILL DO IT"

We count, of course, because we're human, and as humans, we want to know that we can beat the snowstorm as well as the cancer prognosis. We count because the Mount Everest we face has not yet fully defied us—we'll take it on like a wasp dodging one swat and coming at it again. Next time we'll do it faster, next time without oxygen, next time blind or at eighty years old or with no legs.[7] Yesterday Louis Zamperini endured forty-seven days in a raft; tomorrow someone else will reach forty-eight.

Yes, there is a measure of self-reliance in our efforts. Why wouldn't there be? But it doesn't need to replace God. In fact, it can't, and this is the other reason we count. As was said above, hope is more than this. The five-Mississippi happens *because* we can't reach the destination on our own. It's a humble place, not a driven place. There is where we feel smaller than the challenge before us, and we know that any self-raised effort will be insufficient in completing the task. It has less to do with sheer willpower and using hope as a verb than it does with surrender and using hope as a noun. I *have* hope.

How do we know there is an immovable object worthy of our confident expectation? How do we know—as the apostle Paul prayed for the Ephesians—the hope to which God has called us (Ephesians 1:18)? It's because of what David Willis calls "the unfolding realization of God's steadfast love."[8] God's love—unfolding over time and proving itself repeatedly—is being realized along the way by all who need it.

In Ezekiel 36, God promised to restore his people. It takes about a dozen verses to list the ways he planned to do it, including physical, spiritual, personal, and communal. Part of it reads like this: "I will gather you from all the countries and bring you back into your own land. I will sprinkle clean water on you, and you will be clean; I will cleanse you from all your impurities and from all your idols. I will give you a new heart and put a new spirit in you. . . . I the LORD have spoken, and I will do it" (vv. 24-26, 36).

Everything here sounds good. But at the time it was given, it was too early to know whether God would come through or how he'd do it. Since we have the benefit of living in Ezekiel's future, we know that supporting evidence came soon enough when the Israelites were freed from their exile in Babylon and sent home with their captors' favor. God fulfilled that part of the promise—to bring them back. Yet he wasn't done.

The content of Ezekiel 36 extended beyond immediate needs. God promised restoration in the sixth century BC, but he also promised the "unfolding"—or increase—of it over time. "Then the nations around you that remain will know that I the LORD have rebuilt what was destroyed and have replanted what was desolate" (v. 36). Their healing would invite others to be healed.

Continuing on, we enter the temple in Jerusalem six hundred years later and see Mary and Joseph with their baby. Here Willis translates the proclamation in Ezekiel 36 by saying, "God fulfills his own promises in person. Jesus Christ is where promise and actualization are personally united." Simeon holds the child and praises God.

> For my eyes have seen your salvation, which you have prepared in the sight of all nations: a light for revelation to the Gentiles, and the glory to your people Israel. (Luke 2:30-32)

Simeon recognizes that God is still doing what he said he would do, and he acknowledges the expansion of the promise. God will heal Israel *and* the Gentiles.

Why is this important in a chapter on growing in hope? Because we need to see that the beliefs we profess have validity. We want to know that God will come through and that waiting is worth it. Otherwise, we're liable to take matters into our own hands or to quit before we actually need to take a breath.

My friend Christopher lost his good job a couple of winters ago and believed he could replace it in less than four months. His plan was confident and methodical: "Network, get referrals, tell potential employers what I have to offer." Those four months

WE WANT TO KNOW THAT GOD WILL COME THROUGH AND THAT WAITING IS WORTH IT.

passed. Then another four—and another four. Nothing but deadends. A year into it, he courted a company for yet another four months. It would be a dream job, a perfect fit—but he got beat out. Rejection again.

A mutual friend and I sat down with him to see how he was doing. He said transparently, "I know our jobs aren't where we're supposed to find our worth, guys, but when you go through this for this long, it really screws with your identity. It affects how you interact with God, with your family, with your community. It's hard coming home from another missed lead and sitting at the table with nothing to say."

Simeon, the man who greeted Mary and Joseph as they brought Jesus into the temple for the first time, builds our confidence. He reminds us to keep watching, and we see God's promise unfold in Mark 5 when Jesus sent a man's demons into a herd of pigs. Jesus said to him, "'Go home to your own people and tell them how much the Lord has done for you, and how he has had mercy on you.' So the man went away and began to tell in the Decapolis how much Jesus had done for him. And all the people were amazed" (vv. 19-20).

Only Gentiles raised pigs, so we know who Jesus was reaching out to. Second, the Decapolis was ten cities of Greek and Roman culture—Gentile cities. There was Jesus, bringing ancient promises to fruition by healing foreigners. Our history with God was gaining momentum.

When the Holy Spirit came at Pentecost, the booming number of followers emerged as the church. The inclusion of Gentiles as fellow light-bearers of God's work took on world-shifting implications as the church grew far beyond the Decapolis to the ends of the known world. Today we confirm with Paul that "the gospel is bearing fruit and growing throughout the world—just as it has been doing among you since the day you heard it and truly understood God's grace" (Colossians 1:6).

How do we know that God keeps his promises? Because he "draws potential reality forward into actualized reality," Willis said.[9] We see it happen, and the resulting faith becomes "the assurance of things hoped for" (Hebrews 11:1 ESV). For Christopher, it would take a full year and a half before the job offer came in. Every day until then, he got up, got dressed, and drove to a coffee shop "to see what might happen." He was expectant, even if frustrated. The daily routine "kept me from going batty," he said. And he recognized the power of community. "The deeper the support network, the better, and yet it didn't take much. For me, even one person helped."

When I asked what happened to his original plan, the self-confident plan, he didn't turn to a trial-tested list of personal accomplishments. Instead, he confessed, "In the end, this job came unexpectedly. It was outside of my doing."

This is what the kingdom of God is like. A man scatters seed on the ground. Night and day, whether he sleeps or gets up, the seed sprouts and grows, though he does not know how. All by itself the soil produces grain—first the stalk, then the head, then the full kernel in the head. (Mark 4:26-28)

Let us hold unswervingly to the hope we profess, for he who promised is faithful. (Hebrews 10:23)

DO IT: DESIGNS TO GROW IN HOPE

God said to Ezekiel, "I will do it." Rarely is this a tomorrow-at-two-thirty kind of promise. But it happens nonetheless. Seeing God act over time helps us to hold on, because it provides faith for hope to feed on. Below are a few basic designs intended for practice and aimed to mature your belief in the hope that God *will*.

Hold your breath. Freediving expert Kirk Krack taught Tom Cruise how to hold his breath for six minutes for *Mission: Impossible—Rogue Nation*. The point for you and me isn't to star in a movie or to break a record.[10] The point is to learn to hold on when you want to quit. Any pool, lake, or ocean will do. Just have a buddy along. Then connect your new feat with an area of life where you're struggling for resolution.

Connection: "Do I believe God will provide?"

Grow a tomato. You don't need a big yard (or any yard) to plant one; sun and water will suffice for the hanging variety. You already know tomatoes can grow, but *will yours*? A neighbor will be happy to make BLTs from your crop if tomatoes aren't your thing. Give the plant a name related to your situation, and each time you pick from it, ask the following question.

Connection: "Do I believe God will produce fruit from my commitment to wait?"

Let them go. Releasing someone you love is never easy. Whether it's because of a romantic breakup, a terminal illness, or a teenager leaving home, separation tears us. Write a letter of gratitude for your own keeping. Thank the Lord for how this person has challenged you and blessed you. Praise God for how he or she raised new questions you hadn't considered and how you matured through the relationship, no matter how difficult or wonderful it was. Pen these words: "I am letting you go."

Connection: "Do I believe God will see both of us through this?"

Keep a routine. Huh? I've been saying to break routine, but this is different. Good habits are good, as you know, especially if a lot of your life is presently in chaos. During Christopher's unemployment, he struggled not being able to provide for his family. At the same time, his wife contracted a serious case of Lyme disease, and they were back home living with family, being told that he should lower his expectations. Daily practices helped keep him grounded.

Connection: "Do I believe God will answer my prayer?"

GROWING IN LOVE

Experiments in Service

On one memorable spring-break trip, students and I spent several full days in Washington, DC, with educational visits, readings and discussions, and stimulating appointments. We met with probation officers, psychologists, displaced residents, and a mix of others, each time asking a simple question: "How do people search for home?"

We wanted to know what drives one elderly woman to hoard and a young man to join a gang; why the seventeen-year old sells her body and a family wants to discover its genealogical roots. Specifically, we wanted to know what about the quest causes our behaviors to conflict with our beliefs. As the hosts responded to our curiosity, we were amazed by the consistency in their answers. "We're looking for love," they said. "And we'll pay any price to get it."

Young, old, black, white, rich, poor, female, male, atheist, Christian—it made no difference. It's the same for everyone: *we need love.* The thing most required by the two great commandments is the thing most required by the human race. What we're asked to give, we need. Love is the summary of the Scriptures, not a generic principle handy for religious calendars. It's the promise of things to come, the missional catalyst of the New Testament church, and the bread and butter of daily living. Love is what binds us to neighbors and keeps us from killing them. Without love, everything falls apart, from political regimes to personal relationships. "And now these three remain: faith, hope and love. But the greatest of these is love" (1 Corinthians 13:13).

This is all well and good, but Jesus has to tell me—*tell* me—to give away the greatest, because I need more than a suggestion. I need the imperative. He also has to tell me because I need a command counter to what I already do so well: love myself. That direction needs no encouragement for me. Guidance, yes; encouragement, no. I love myself in abundance—readily and recklessly.

With our urban observations in mind, we left DC and drove to a remote wilderness area in Virginia to reflect on what we had experienced. (Reflection, as I've said above and will return to in more detail in chapter seven, is a critical follow-up to every experience.) The city had been comfortable: working appliances, light, heat, water, electricity, comfy couches, locked doors, restaurants, and grocery stores. Now it was time to remove those comforts and see how we would do. If kids join gangs to cope with lack in the city, would we show similar tendencies when coping with lack in the woods? Where we were headed, the trails were unmarked, and it was half a mile from our tent site to the trickling stream where we hoped to find water. That type of scenario can make people behave strangely.

At dusk, four hours west of the capital and now standing at a trailhead wearing boots and heavy packs, we said goodbye to cars and predictability and began the three-and-a-half-mile ascent. Hours later—our headlamps having kept us on the path—we finally reached the isolated clearing along the ridge. Under normal circumstances, it wouldn't have been a difficult hike, but with no daylight and after busy days with constant mental exercise and late nights (not to mention that we hadn't eaten dinner), it was rather tiring.

I didn't have the luxury of resting any time soon. The temperature had dropped below freezing, and I had to think about getting everyone fed and keeping them warm. It requires considerable energy to set up camp and cook dinner in the dark, especially when it's cold and especially with first-time hikers who don't know enough about the wild to pee without instructions.

Conditions like this also tend to foster unusual issues. One student, for example, doubled over with an inexplicable pain that lasted through the evening. Another pulled me aside to say he was experiencing the onset of an anxiety attack. These would both subside as confidence increased. But they exacerbated the situation at hand.

With numb fingers, we created a shelter by tying a thick plastic tarp to nearby trees. Dinner was prepared over pocketsize camping stoves. It was a simple meal, but even boiled bark would have satisfied at that point. I coached participants on what to wear for bed, and then several of us went farther into the woods to hang food bags and cookware in trees so bears couldn't reach them. Sometime after midnight, I zipped up my sleeping bag. I was beat. The anxious participant asked quietly if he could wake me during the night if an attack came. I hoped that either he'd be fine or I'd sleep through his request.

This unspoken response from me was the first clear break from love. The next would come less than an hour later.

A sound of desperation jarred me awake. It was Miriam, a student three sleeping bags away from my resting place. She had bolted upright and was now gasping for air and calling out in a panic. Students beside her tried to assist, but what were they to do?

All she could say was that she had stopped breathing. Just stopped. Everyone was now awake and scared, and they asked me what to do. I didn't care. I hadn't even rolled over yet—only turned my head enough to see the commotion in my peripheral vision. I wanted to tell her, "Lie back down, and we'll deal with your problems in the morning." Of course, that wasn't an option, though I so wanted it to be. I was beyond caring and starving for sleep.

These are the moments when Jesus-like attributes we've collected over the years fail to show up. No Sunday school lessons come shining through. No spiritual wisdom from parents and peers save the day. No, this is when immaturity says, "Responsibility? Adulthood? Giving your life away? I don't think so. I'm the one who counts. I'm going back to sleep."

In a fortuitous moment of clarity, I remembered that Miriam suffered from exercise-induced asthma. She was an athlete with a high tolerance; that's why, in all of our activities that week, I had forgotten about it. Now a mental picture of her medical form popped into view. When I learned that she had cinched up her sleeping bag hole and created a cocoon (producing too much humidity), I leaned on my elbow and asked her to try keeping her head out in the cold instead. It worked, and I can't tell you how glad I was.

I don't need encouragement to love myself. I'm a pro at it. What I need is to love my neighbor. That tiresome night put me exactly where I had hoped it would put the students—in a place of shortage and challenge so they could observe where they still needed to mature. Yet it was me who was making the observations.

Home is stuff like shelter, rest, and companionship. It's that place where love is healthy and abundant and where all the good promises of God come to fruition. Entering a designed experience in the wilderness removes the ability to control how we get these good items. Participants feel threatened as they wonder not only how they'll survive the frozen night but also what lives in the shadows and how to cook without a microwave. Perceived threats lead to all manner of unpredictable responses, and the responses show us our immaturity.

It's one thing to hear strangers talk about hungering for home in a warm, well-lit conference room in DC but quite another to feel these hungers yourself on a wintry night in the middle of nowhere. There I was, subjected to the design I had created for others. My need was rest, and the more endangered my rest became, the more negatively I responded to those who threatened it.

> MY NEED WAS REST, AND THE MORE ENDANGERED REST BECAME, THE MORE NEGATIVELY I RESPONDED TO THOSE WHO THREATENED IT.

When I suffer, my willingness (and ability) to love my neighbor suffers, too.

LOVE IN THE DARK

How can I reach a level of maturity at which personal suffering doesn't hinder my love for others? In other words, what does it look like when love is working? This is an ancient question. It's also fundamentally a question about becoming more human, for when we act in the love of God, we act in the way we were made to act. James wrote that maturity is synonymous with not lacking anything (James 1:4). The opposite is equally true: immaturity is synonymous with lack.

One could argue that every sin ever committed happened because the perpetrator couldn't handle this or that unmet desire, beginning with Adam and Eve. Then came Cain, who couldn't handle what he perceived as a lack of love and took it out on his brother. History proves that we fail at persevering through challenges. Henri Nouwen puts it bluntly: "When our unfulfilled needs lead us to demand from our fellow human beings what they cannot give, we make them into idols and ourselves into devils. By asking for more than a human response we are tempted to behave as less than human."[1]

What keeps us from giving in altogether? Grace, absolutely. Willpower, to a degree. Peer pressure, laws, moral convictions. And, for sure, inspiration. Rubbing shoulders with people who live like Jesus inspires us to do the same. Their examples of super-human sacrifice keep us from throwing in the towel. I've picked the following story because (1) it contrasts the story above, (2) I was present for both, and (3) both created space for me to reflect differently on the same topic.

I met Juancito in 2011. He was immensely shy and equally short in stature, and his contagious smile made him grander than he appeared. Miguel, the lead guide for our five-day trek to the ancient Incan ruins of Choquequirao in South America,[2] introduced him as our cook, and we were told that he was excellent at his job. It didn't take long to confirm that. Juancito was like the waiter who swoops in with a fresh drink seconds before you realized you need one.

In the outdoors, I've enjoyed campfire-baked pepperoni rolls, Cajun Spam melts, and powdered milk tea with vanilla and cinnamon. But I had never *dined* in the wilderness until I met Juancito. Three meals per day, four courses per meal, sometimes in an off-trail clearing, sometimes in the corner of an empty cinder-block room, he quietly prepared savory, satisfying food for our group and the guide team, and he kept it coming until long after we were full.

As the cook, this was his job; we paid him to do it. But I had been paid for my services on that chilly spring break in Virginia too. He created a menu; I created the itinerary for a backpacking trip. He prepared meals in the middle of nowhere; I prepared a campsite in the middle of nowhere. He kept us fed; I kept us safe. What struck me about Juancito was that he did his job more generously than I did mine. He got up earlier, hiked faster, worked longer hours, and went to bed later. Picture it: he had to clean up each meal after we left camp, then get to the next meal site miles away before we arrived in order to have another multicourse meal ready for us. He had no access to a road or shortcut. He just had to move at double our pace. And whereas my trip in the Virginia mountains topped out at a measly 3,400 feet above sea level, his cooking in the Andes took place in the oxygen-thin atmosphere above ten thousand. In so many ways, he outdid me, and I was impressed. But it was what happened next that really made me pause.

One evening, after eleven hours of hiking, I stumbled along a horse path beyond the tents to brush my teeth. I could hear the tiny mountain stream to my left, but otherwise was deep in thought about the day, when I became aware of a dim light ahead. As I approached the place where the water came out of an embankment through a pipe, I could tell that the light belonged to someone with his or her back to me.

I continued forward and saw that a man was kneeling beneath the pipe with a large sack open at his side. It was Juancito. He was washing our dishes in the stream: pots, pans, ladles, plates, silverware, and pitchers for more than twenty people. I tried to say good night or thank you or anything to acknowledge him there, but I couldn't. He had not heard me over the sound of the water nor had he seen me in the dark, so I stared, several feet away, like a voyeur, unable to ignore that he was doing something beyond my imagination. I used the darkness to slip away.

Over the next few days, I paid attention to Juancito. I wanted to know—for my own selfish preservation of dignity—when this guy would break. I also wanted to know what impact this humble servant would have on our group. Lewis Hyde writes, "In folk tales the gift is often something seemingly worthless—ashes or coals or leaves or straw—but when the puzzled recipient carries it to his doorstep, he finds it has turned to gold. Such tales declare that the motion of the gift from the world of the donor to the doorsill of the recipient is sufficient to transmute it from dross to gold."[3]

As the week progressed, gold began to emerge as the students affirmed Juancito. They praised him for his amazing food, and though their hesitant taste buds caused them to reject the stranger dishes, he knew they tried. His smile—his own gold—grew. By the end, Juancito's name entered nearly every conversation, and the students begged, "Can we *please* take you home with us?" He was no longer simply our cook. Their attention and respect flattered him, and on the eve of the last day—in his quiet manner and with knowledge that the predawn alarm for another day of rigorous cooking and hiking would come soon—he labored past midnight to bake us a cake.

Hyde wrote that "when you give a gift there is momentum."[4] He called this the increase. "The increase is the core of the gift. . . . In gift exchange it, the increase, stays in motion and follows the object, while in commodity exchange it stays behind as profit."[5] There is the exchange of goods and services (represented by the contract we entered for Juancito's services), and then there is the increase. As Jesus liked to say in so many analogous ways, the increase is what characterizes the kingdom.

When Miriam struggled to breath, I experienced what love should *not* look like. When I watched Juancito cleaning dishes in ice-cold water with a few stones as his drying rack, I witnessed what it should look like. And I watched the momentum of his gift increase with each meal and every interaction.

It may be true that I'm selfish and short on sacrifice, but I can recognize a lesson when God sends one my way. I was sufficiently convicted that from then on I curbed my complaints and pushed harder. I got up when I wanted to stay seated. I offered help when I wanted somebody else to do it. I'm grateful for this, for it resurrected a part of me.

Pharaoh himself was dead long before his firstborn was taken, for we are only alive to the degree that we can let ourselves be moved. And when the gift circles into mystery the liveliness stays, for it is "a pleasing odor to the Lord" when the first fruits are effused in eddies and drifted in lacy jags above the flame.[6]

The challenge was to continue fostering that increase in my life after the experience.

THE GRIP OF ME FIRST

Selfishness is tough to break away from. Get to work on it with the help of other people. For example, contact an organization like L.I.V.I.N.G. Ministry (livingministry.org) to schedule an experience with your church staff, youth group, or college fellowship. They serve the homeless on the street and can facilitate custom designs so you can do something more challenging than serving meals.

MOVING ON FROM SELF-CENTEREDNESS

Of the three—faith, hope, and love—"the greatest of these" is the weakest of mine. Juancito proved to be a gentle nudge toward maturity in this area, because he continued where I stopped. Author Ronald Rolheiser suggests that we can't really love as Jesus loves until we pass through the first and most self-centered stage of our lives.[7] In those early years, perhaps lasting into our mid-twenties or mid-thirties, we obsess over questions such as "Am I loved?" and "Where do I belong?" The questions don't necessarily go away in our forties, but the piecemeal answers we gained then form the support we need later. Lifeguards know about this kind of development. Without good training—without maturity—we can't take care of others well. Drowning people can't save drowning people.

Self-focused questions early on ironically become critical in developing our service to others. If I know who I am, what role I play, where I matter, who needs me, and so on, the answers collectively form a base that allows me to reach outward. But the progression isn't linear. In some areas, I showed maturity long before answering the questions; in others, I answered the questions decades ago but still act like I'm five. The problem may involve a conundrum with self-centeredness: we are on one hand physiologically self-centered, which is critical for survival, while on the other we are spiritually called to deny ourselves and even lay down our lives for our friends (1 John 3:16). The two have trouble coexisting.

Physiologically, for instance, the brain must serve itself. Let's say I get injured in a car accident (I did). The brain initiates a series of steps to preserve itself as blood loss occurs. This process cannot be stopped. First, it tells my body to constrict its vessels to mimic normal blood pressure as volume decreases. It even makes me pass out or feel like I want to, which causes me to fall down or lie down (the EMT caught me the second time), so the brain does not have to fight with gravity. It wants to eliminate any and all opposition.

My situation wasn't too serious, but here's what would have happened if it were: my brain would have begun cutting off resources to what it deemed less important—first skin (this is why we turn pale before passing out), then muscles, then the stomach and intestines, liver, kidneys, and eventually lungs. These shutdown measures would have permitted my brain to keep my heart going, even at a severely diminished state. It would have turned off my heart too, but a pumping heart supplies essential oxygen to the brain. The brain is king, and if the king ain't happy, ain't nobody happy.

Spiritually speaking, I don't get an excuse to turn off someone because I could use a nap or because I'm running late for work or because I don't feel like doing the dishes in the creek in the dark by myself after a long day. I don't have the moral privilege of taking care of myself first and then, after recovering, decide to be generous again. I'm not allowed to follow my brain's lead. Instead, maturity looks more like the call of St. Ignatius of Loyola, when he stated daringly, "Thus, as far as we are concerned, we should not want health more than illness, wealth more than poverty, fame more than disgrace, a long life more than a short one, and similarly for all the rest, but we should desire and choose only what helps us more towards the end for which we are created."[8]

Ugh. This sounds nothing like the natural, physiological response of the brain to hard times. It's more like a sadistic request for suffering: "If bleeding will help me care for others, Lord, then so be it." It's crazy talk, and it's confusing because I agree with the flight attendant who orders me to put on my oxygen mask before helping you with yours. She isn't promoting a me-first catering service, but wisdom. Oxygen-deprived people can't save oxygen-deprived people. And yet the tales of service that get passed along for generations are those that involve giving out of shortage. It is not the abundance of the wealthy that inspires us but the sacrifice of the poor.

In 1 Kings, the prophet Elijah meets a widow at Zarephath. When Elijah asks her to bring him water and a piece of bread, she replies, "I don't have any bread—only a handful of flour in a jar and a little olive oil in a jug. I am gathering a few sticks to take home and make a meal for myself and my son, that we may eat it—and die" (17:12). Lewis Hyde spoke of the increase in gift exchange, and we see it in what happens next: despite the widow's situation, "she went away and did as Elijah had told her. So there was food every day for Elijah and for the woman and her family. For the jar of flour was not used up and the jug of oil did not run dry, in keeping with the word of the LORD spoken by Elijah" (vv. 15-16).

Did I need sleep that night in the woods? Yes. Did I have a right to disregard my frightened camper? No. Of course, there are certain moments—reasonable moments—when giving out of shortage really is foolish. I should not try to rescue you from a burning building once it begins to cave in. I should not perform surgery on you (if I knew how) if I've been awake for three days. These actions would cause more harm than good. And yet I read of the widow's service to Elijah, and I don't know what to think.

I do know this: there is a gap between when I *want* to stop serving and when I *ought* to stop serving. It will feel like a stretch to close that gap, but only because it's pushing me past perceived limits, not actual limits. How else will I learn? Perseverance doesn't finish its work in theory; it finishes its work in practice.

> **PERSEVERANCE DOESN'T FINISH ITS WORK IN THEORY; IT FINISHES ITS WORK IN PRACTICE.**

CLOSING THE GAP

Several high school students asked our church group to support their hunger awareness program. It was a fast that stretched from midnight on Friday until noon on Sunday, during which they performed service projects around the city and slept in cardboard boxes in the cold. (That's a great disruptive experience, by the way.)

I was struck by one student in particular. Instead of promoting the event and asking us to help reach the donation goal, Hoa said, "This is my fourth year doing this. I'm a senior in high school, and it amazes me that we have to schedule an event just to remember that people have so many hard things going on in their lives."

I thought, *Even if I found the courage to close my service gap, serving one time wouldn't be enough. If I don't practice on a regular basis, I'll slip back into comfort.* Isn't this the point of designed experiences? They force us to practice perseverance, so that even when we are bleeding out—metaphorically speaking—we still have room for generosity.

Hoa and her friends left the room, but her words stayed behind. Despite needing an annual reminder, I imagine that because of her experience she has grown in a number of ways toward love, much more so than someone without her experience. The following came to mind:

- For four years, Hoa has spent at least one day volunteering at a different location. This means interacting with socioeconomic strangers, recognizing and remembering her own privilege, and learning from the host sites about how various organizations function.

- Stepping into another's shoes has probably taught Hoa to see her own "homelessness," a reflection that's important in becoming other-centered. Rolheiser wrote, "A mature person watching the news at night and seeing the world's wars, violence, and wounds responds with empathy because she already recognizes within herself that same complexity, neediness, pride, greed, and lust that lie at the root of all that unrest. Deep maturity is very much synonymous with empathy."[9]

- Based on the significant amount of money she and her friends raise for this cause each year, I also imagined that Hoa has seen her ability to make a difference (a real boost in self-worth) and that there is tremendous power in serving the community *as* a community. After all, she could have stayed home by herself to watch movies and sleep in a warm bed.

- I didn't have to imagine that her awareness has developed a conviction to tell others about loving neighbors. I could see it. Hoa was on the promotion team to make announcements in each of a dozen or more classrooms, and then she reported in front of the entire congregation afterward about how the event turned out.

The more we mature, the more we love. Rolheiser quoted Teresa of Ávila to confirm this progression: "When one reaches the highest degree of human maturity, one has only one question left: How can I be helpful?"[10] Just hearing the question reminds me of my immaturity, and I want to be transformed from a self-absorbed child into a generous adult.

It helps knowing that love is an extension of faith and hope; it's an outward manifestation of my inward beliefs. Faith believes that God can, hope believes that God will, and love demonstrates this belief in action. It's like the first time my daughter Emma got on a grownup roller coaster. She had no idea what to expect, but she got in because I was next to her. The buckle and bar helped, but I was the closest representation of the assurance of things hoped for. As we gained speed, terror overcame her. What did she do? She let go of the bar and wrapped her arms around me. Her face was the picture of fear.

One turn, two turns, the first dip and the second, I talked all the while about what was coming and what she had accomplished. She had no ability to do anything but search for anchors. When we finally neared the end, her grip lessened. I helped her out of the car and said, "You did it! What do you think of that?" to which she said, to my surprise, "I want to get back in line right now."

We did, and I watched the shift occur from self-focus to other-focus as she invited her younger sister and cousins to take their first rides, saying, "You can ride with me." It isn't possible to love well without a foundation of faith and hope.

As we close part two, remember that growth is nonlinear. You may read an email today that challenges your status quo. Instead of being able to progress to the next stage of maturity, you'll need to return to ground you just covered—only now with ears to hear in a fresh way. That's how it works: we grow in an area until we meet a challenge we haven't met before. Then it's back to praying for maturity and looking for solutions. It's a cycle with fits and starts, despite maintaining a general pattern of experiencing (planned or unplanned), translating, transferring, and integrating—a pattern we will look at more closely in the next chapter. From learning to ride a bicycle to breaking away from that codependent relationship, the student within us keeps going.

I'm convinced that the practice of disrupting routine on purpose makes the road to maturity less choppy, less up and down. If that sounds counterintuitive, that's because it is. The disruptions develop a steadiness, the kind you observe in someone who has weathered a few storms. Who was more freaked out—pre-roller coaster Emma or post-roller coaster Emma?

But we aren't interested in amusement-park challenges if the experience remains isolated. As a disciple (and as a disciple maker of my daughter), I want those challenges to find their way into the rest of life. I want them to convert into a faith, a hope, and a love that makes the unexpected email a little less threatening. It's the steadiness we want, not the chop.

Part three will address several application topics, including how to integrate lessons from an experience into everyday living, how to deal with unwelcome experiences (as well as learning to deny ourselves when they come), and how to keep from getting stuck so often.

DO IT: DESIGNS TO GROW IN LOVE

We know by small gestures and by costly sacrifice how it feels to be loved. Love preserves us. It reaches beyond our sense of worth and heals us. It also confronts us, because in God's economy, love isn't satisfied with letting us stay where we are. As we have received (or as we have desired to receive), we now attempt to give to others. The following designs range from easy to difficult and aim to develop actions that demonstrate our beliefs. Pick one and give it a go.

Make the most of being self-centered. Then move on. You may need a coach or other mentor to accompany you—people who know you subjectively and objectively. Ask for help with questions like "Who am I?" "What role do I play?" and "Who needs me?" It's okay if the answers change over time. That happens with maturity. For now, seek honest responses, and trust what you hear so you can serve with less *you* in the way.

Connection: "How does self-focus affect my love for others?"

Relinquish first dibs. Maybe you've experienced it at summer camp or in a college residence hall, at a conference or a hunting cabin—anywhere rooms are shared: the early arriver takes the best bunk. It's a seemingly inconsequential act, but behind it lies a selfish disregard for others. Be the servant leader. Wait until your roommate arrives, and then offer the best to him or her. It may cost in short-term comfort, but the rewards are great over time. Try other first-dib surrendering to test your love: the last piece of dark-chocolate peppermint Bundt cake, riding shotgun, setting the Spotify channel.

Connection: "What is at stake if I put others before me?"

Go and do likewise. Read Luke 10:25-37. Consider how Jesus might retell the story with you, in your profession, as the good Samaritan. As an engineer, how could you help the situation? Maybe reroute the road to safer ground for future travelers? If you teach, could you take a position in the neighborhood that produced the thieves? As a counselor, could you aid the beaten man through potential post-traumatic stress? Then take Jesus literally and vocationally in your modern-day context and "go and do likewise" (v. 37).

Connection: "How can my training be better employed in service?"

Give someone a day. Write twenty-five names of people you know on a sheet of paper. Include friends, family members, and neighbors, a few acquaintances, and at least one person you don't like. Cut the names from the sheet and place them in a bowl. Without looking, draw a name. Now pick a date on the calendar and commit it to that person. The theme could be celebration or service, education or reconciliation, but the time must be spent with or directly for that individual.

Connection: "Do I love my neighbor as myself?"

Part Three

GROWING

UP

TRANSLATING CHANGE

7

We had the experience but missed the meaning.

T. S. Eliot

Francis Chan uses a humorous way to describe how *not* to be a disciple:

> When I tell my daughter, "Hey, Rach, go clean your room," she doesn't come back to me two hours later and go, "I memorized what you said. You said, 'Rach, go clean your room.' I can say it in Greek. My friends are going to come over and we're going to have a study on what it would look like if I cleaned my room."[1]

He's comparing discipleship to the childhood game "Simon Says," in which you perform whatever simple task the leader tells you to perform. If Simon says, "Simon says, 'Turn around,'" you turn around. But Chan observes that we adopt different rules when it comes to following Jesus: "If Jesus says something, you don't have to do it, you just have to memorize it."[2]

What good are examples and instructions if they remain examples and instructions? Remember Juancito, the backpacking cook? I had to do something with that experience. If the increase of his hospitality stopped when I returned home from that trip, I'd be guilty of stopping the momentum of the gift and therefore the benefits of its increase. "Go and do likewise," Jesus said (Luke 10:37).

In a workshop called Five Reasons You Should Travel and Come Back Again, we wanted to encourage college students and young professionals to use this time of relatively disposable income and low responsibility to get out and see the world. The point was not to add stamps to their passports, but to inspire them to become better neighbors. G. K. Chesterton wrote, "If we were tomorrow morning snowed up in the street in which we live, we should step suddenly into a much larger and much wilder world than we have ever known."[3]

Why start a travel workshop with this line about living right next door? Because travel opens new doors for growth. Going *far* challenges our assumptions about living *near*. It suspends normal and causes us either to become bolder in the absence of comfort or to shut down. Either way, we must, as Allie discovered on the bus in Peru, deal with our presuppositions about God, ourselves, and the world that normally remains hidden from view.

It's easy to keep these hidden, because the nearby world is so familiar that we can manage it with great dexterity. Visiting a foreign place throws off everything, forcing us to question what we take for granted and to reassess what we thought we valued. When we return, we are more likely to see what we've been ignoring on our own street—like discovering that I love Latino families in Mexico but neglect to talk to them in my grocery store in the United States.

If Chesterton is right—that the world really opens up next door—reaching out to people who live thousands of miles away may make sense as an elementary step toward aligning our local behaviors with our deepest beliefs. For one, it's more exotic, even if colder or more desolate than home. More importantly, it's more romantic, perhaps even more preferred. Next door (the word *neighbor* comes from *near* plus *dwellers*) is usually trickier. Consider this convicting description, again by Chesterton:

> We make our friends; we make our enemies; but God makes our next-door neighbor. Hence he comes to us clad in all the careless terrors of nature; he is as strange as the stars, as reckless and indifferent as the rain. . . . That is why the old religions and the old scriptural language showed so sharp a wisdom when they spoke, not of one's duty toward humanity, but one's duty toward one's neighbor. The duty toward humanity may often take the form of some choice which is personal or even pleasurable. That duty may be a hobby; it may even be a dissipation. We may work in the East End because we are peculiarly fitted to work in the East End, or because we think we are; we may fight for the cause of international peace because we are very fond of fighting. The most monstrous martyrdom, the most repulsive experience, may be the result of choice or a kind of taste. We may be so made as to be particularly fond of lunatics or specially interested in leprosy. . . . But we have to love our neighbor because he is there—a much more alarming reason for a much more serious operation.[4]

Chesterton pits "duty toward humanity" against "duty toward one's neighbor." It's hobby versus obligation. Do you see why travel might be considered a good step toward the real stuff of next-door living? Travel has options; near-dwelling does not. Travel is a privilege and offers pleasure; near-dwelling is a duty and can feel like work. I encourage travel because it promotes healthier day-to-day living where it counts: back at home—the physical place of residence as well as the familiar contexts where we live out the gospel in lasting ways. It's the cubicle and the local diner that need our souvenirs.

In this chapter, let's focus on the return home and how to integrate designed experiences into our everyday lives.

TRANSLATION, TRANSFERENCE, AND INTEGRATION

Translation. Translation is the act of discerning meaning. We translate foreign languages (except when my taxi driver in Lima talks so fast I just smile and pray that we find the right address). We also translate difficult concepts. When my daughters were young, they didn't need to know about amperes, molecular friction, and skin cells. They only needed to know that the stove was hot.

And we translate personal experiences. One night, while a group was backpacking in Kentucky, a woman began to exhibit signs of shock. As we explored potential causes, none of my questions produced an answer. The following morning, she was fine. After dinner, the signs and symptoms returned. How would you have translated what was going on with her? (As it turned out, she was afraid of the dark.)

Translation helps us interpret the unfamiliar, whether it's in a physics class or in the backyard when the grass dies in patches every September. (Probably grubs.) Translation helps us in these ways because it is a form of reflection. You've had an experience—however far away—and now you're making sense of it by reflecting on it.

Transference. Transference is the necessary follow-up to translation. Transference involves connecting the meaning we discover in one part of life to a need in another part of life. Emma rode a roller coaster. So what? The lesson in that ride (assuming there was one) should find a home beyond the amusement park. Otherwise, who cares what she learned from it? The translation won't matter if the meaning isn't carried over.

TRANSLATION QUESTIONS

Recently, I was asked to colead a trip that ministered to homeless people—not serving food, but actually spending time with them on the street. I didn't want to. The homeless scare me, and I feel judgmental around them, which is precisely how I knew I needed to sign up. The following sample questions are based on meeting a seventy-two-year-old man named Ed, who lived under a tarp.

Questions I asked myself:

- What just happened?

- What am I feeling now—judgmental, sad, afraid, peaceful?

- Why was this experience more different than I thought it would be?

Questions you could ask me after I told you about meeting Ed (if not the ones I asked myself):

- What happened, Sam? What was it like?

- What made you treat him with hospitality?

One of my painfully favorite examples of translation and transference happened on the TV show *Wipeout*. A contestant ran across the platform and got blasted backward by a hidden door. She promptly stood up, ran forward in the same direction on the same platform, and got blasted a second time by the same hidden door. What happened next? She did the same thing a third time. Same direction, same platform, same hidden door, same blast. She must have translated what was going on, but she definitely didn't transfer any of the meaning.

That contestant's failure to act differently after the first attempt astounds me, but then I remember that earlier that day I chose anger over patience. It got me nowhere yesterday or last week, so what made me think it would work today? Immaturity is pockmarked by indications of insanity, making transference critical.

In higher education. Higher education institutions have a type of student walking their halls that resembles this contestant, though, to be fair, it isn't exactly the student's fault. He's been over-parented. Parents who hover like helicopters, or clear paths like bulldozers, have been the culprit not only in protecting children from hardship but in becoming the reason behind a host of college programs aimed at "unparenting" students. These post–high schoolers suffer from a form of learned helplessness caused by in-lieu decision making, and one result is a delay in consequential thinking. In other words, they have trouble with transference. "If I don't have to think for myself," one of them might say, "I don't have to deal with the results either." Accustomed to being handed solutions without having to work through the problems, this student struggles to connect cause and effect. A life of relative ease doesn't require it.

Like many in higher ed, Christy Hanson is attempting to do something about it. Christy is the director of career and professional development at Messiah College, and in 2015 she spearheaded the Experiential Learning Initiative, a program designed to enhance connections between campus life and students' post-college lives.[5] Here's a snapshot of the process:

- Apply for a forty-hour experience (for example, an internship or studying abroad).
- Write outcomes to solidify the reasons behind applying.
- Have the experience.
- Meet throughout the process with an adviser to track progress toward the outcomes.
- Reflect on the outcomes once the experience has ended.

Besides the tangible addition that this process contributes to students' portfolios, a more important benefit exists: it teaches them to make connections.

When I asked Christy if her program was really about experiential learning, as the language suggests, she said, "No, it's really about transference. Our team designed the reflection questions to help students make connections. We want them to think about why the internship, for example, matters to their life, work, and community after college. Right now, very few students know how to do that."

This comment caught my attention. "Don't the connections happen naturally?"

"They don't," she replied. "Again and again, we hear students say things like, 'During my interview, the employer asked what impact studying abroad will have on the position I'm applying for, and I didn't have an answer.' They tell us, 'I just didn't see any connection between the two.'"

Christy is not alone. Schools across the country have introduced experience-based learning programs. In part, they want to help students who are, as Christy told *Huffington Post*, "having a hard time taking the value of [their] experiences beyond the experience itself."[6]

And it isn't only about parents. Schooling that emphasizes information over experiences has been a limiting factor in students' development. Educator and philosopher Paolo Freire likened traditional education to banking, where information is the static deposit in students' accounts. "The more students work at storing the deposits entrusted to them, the less they develop the critical consciousness which would result from their intervention in the world as transformers of that world."[7]

It makes me think of the perennial middle school question about algebra: "What does this have to do with the rest of my life?" Insufficient responses taught us to believe there was no answer (aren't dependent variables and success in school somehow related?), so we stopped asking the question.

In the neighborhood. We lived on welfare for most of my childhood, which means we rarely had enough. At one point, four of us kids shared a single bedroom. We had to share many things, like chairs and bicycles, and the very occasional Snickers bar. I didn't enjoy this level of sharing—fighting over grams or minutes—and yet I find myself in a profession today where forcing people into shared experiences is of fundamental importance. Funny how this happens.

Those years taught me the values associated with sharing, such as communication, sacrifice, hospitality, and interdependence—attributes that now characterize the relationships between my siblings and me as adults. I still prefer having my own stuff, but putting others and myself in situations that dissuade self-orientation has led to good. It's a transference thing. It's a benefit from something as basic as sharing with siblings.

But I'm not done learning yet, as indicated by my occasional desire to wave a magic wand and give every house on our street its own driveway to replace the social dance we experience known as on-street parking. We have no front yard and no more than an arm's reach between houses. This makes snow removal a problem. The bigger the storm, the more risk we face of losing our unofficial yet recognized parking spot, especially when one guy either doesn't know the rules or doesn't care about them. That guy moved in last August.

His name is Hakeem, and he comes and goes at odd hours, taking whatever spot is available. When thirty-five inches of snow fell in one weekend last January, I wondered how things would go down. We piled it high, making cubicle walls around each car, with just enough room for a multipoint exit into traffic once the plows passed. We shoveled for hours, broke for food and sleep, then shoveled again. And we did it together. But Hakeem never came to help. He never joined us; all he did was show up in one or another cleared spaces at unpredictable times.

People go crazy over things like this. *I* was going crazy, thinking, *There's a system here, man!*

I finally decided that if I ran into him, I'd point out, as hospitably as possible, that he had a perfect unofficial spot in front of his place—and would he mind using it? I'd even help dig him out.

Here's what happened when we finally met. I learned that Hakeem is from another country and a very different culture. He goes to school full time and works six nights a week as a forklift trainer. His wife is pregnant, and he is teaching her English (he speaks four languages). So I learned that he doesn't have much room in his life for a shovel. In fact, when I brought up the parking thing, it surprised him. Was he self-centered? Culturally unaware? I don't know. He'd been here only six months.

Hakeem has turned out to be a delightful chap, not at all the enemy I was making him out to be—which brings me back to transference. In the heat of wondering what to do about my neighbor, I longed to wave a magic wand, not work things out. No more stress! No more confrontation! But I was ignoring the lessons gained from childhood. I hadn't transferred them to my neighbor yet.

In the woods. Five student leaders and their campus minister, Mollie, came to the Dolly Sods Wilderness Area before Mollie went on sabbatical. She wanted to prepare them for a semester without her. She knew her role had been very hands-on, so my coworker and I designed a day of orienteering for them. It included two basic rules:

1. The students had to find an off-trail destination using a map and a compass.

2. Mollie had to remain silent for the duration of the exercise.

We began with a lesson and a relatively easy test to assess their collaboration skills. They nearly failed. If it weren't for one particular question asked, they would have wandered off indefinitely. The near-miss revealed a group of individuals, not a group. They sat down apart from each other, and we asked about their observations.

Teamwork could be better, they said. It would certainly need to be for the real assignment, for that involved a mile-and-a-half off-trail hike across streams, brush, pine forest, and rocks, then up and over a ridge, eventually into a partial meadow, where they were to locate one unique tree. We read Jeremiah 6:16:

> This is what the LORD says:
> "Stand at the crossroads and look;
>   ask for the ancient paths,
>   ask where the good way is, and walk in it,
>   and you will find rest for your souls."

And then we took away Mollie's voice.

Now they stood together, calibrated their compasses together, and communicated together. It's amazing how a true challenge (and trepidation) can bind people. And off they went.

About forty-five minutes later, we asked if they knew their location. Confidence varied from wavering to moderate, but we were happy to see them using the tricks and tips from the practice test. They were borrowing faith to bolster hope in the current challenge. So far, so good.

Two components were responsible for doubts, however. First, unlike the practice, which had taken place in the open barrens, this one was full of obstacles. Brush was thick. Gullies were deep. They couldn't see where they had come from. Second, the distance was almost six times as long. Even if they tried to estimate the distance traveled, the difficult terrain would confuse them.

One aspect did work in their favor: they were operating as a team. Conferring with their maps and each other, they agreed that they had reached the headwaters of Red Creek. Where on Red Creek, they weren't quite sure, but they knew beyond a shadow of a doubt that if this were an emergency, they could turn downstream and find Dry Fork, which becomes the Black Fork, which becomes the Cheat River, then the Monongahela River, then the Ohio River, and eventually the Mississippi River.

Suddenly, they weren't lost. This boosted their confidence. In the wilderness, a reference point like this places you in a particular location on a particular map, the topographical equivalent of Jeremiah 6:16. It really is something to say, "I know where I am!"

Through quaking aspens, a beech grove, a patch of delicious wild huckleberries and blueberries, they finally reached the destination. What a mystery to walk so far with so many obstacles and find the one tree among tens of thousands—without GPS and without Google Maps. But that's what they did. And we were glad, because they would need similar navigation skills to tackle the coming semester with no Mollie to guide them. The exercise could be enough to send them on their way with a few tools to put into practice.

Transference, however, is not the same as integration.

TRANSFERENCE QUESTIONS

Here are sample questions based on meeting Ed, who lived under the tarp.

Questions I asked myself:

- What was it about this encounter that challenged my perspective?

- Where else in my life am I stuck behind stereotypes?

Questions you could ask me about meeting Ed (if not the ones I asked myself):

- It sounds like you were surprised by a second impression. Has this happened to you before?

- How does distance from other people's stories keep you from caring?

- What connections do you see between Ed and the man who was beat up in the parable of the good Samaritan?

Integration (and a realistic expectation of lasting change).
The process begins when we make sense of an experience by reflecting on it. That's translation. Then we transfer the meaning to other parts of our lives. "Ah," a student might say, "our performance in this wilderness challenge says a lot about how we function on a regular basis. We've got work to do."

Integration comes next: applying those observations and lessons by putting them into practice. This turns out to be rather difficult. Mollie's student leaders might approach future work more confidently and collaboratively if they integrate what they learned from orienteering into their ministry back on campus (back at "home"). But they may not transfer those lessons at all, and the experience will remain little more than a photo album and a few scrapes and bruises, either because they didn't know they should apply what they learned or because they forgot to do it. The most important aha moments in life have a way of escaping if they aren't firmly attached to a new setting.

> THE MOST IMPORTANT AHA MOMENTS IN LIFE HAVE A WAY OF ESCAPING IF THEY AREN'T FIRMLY ATTACHED TO A NEW SETTING.

Jennifer Dukes Lee's *Love Idol: Letting Go of Your Need for Approval and Seeing Yourself Through God's Eyes* spurred movement among readers when she wrote about seeing yourself as God sees you—behind the makeup and public show. Her book even featured a mirror on the cover. Jennifer is an award-winning journalist, a top-of-the-class kind of writer with hospitality so down-home that friends flock to her.

But how many of those initial followers still have their mirrors covered or out-of-sight? It isn't that they decided one morning that Jennifer's material was irrelevant. On the contrary, they are plagued like all of us with short-term memory for what God has promised to do in our lives (Deuteronomy 8:12-14). Readers of any similarly convicting inspiration will go all-in at first. But you know how it works: we have a stellar first week and then slip in the second week, justifying it by saying, "What's really important is keeping vanity out of it." More frequent slips lead to softer boundaries, which lead to forgetting the vanity piece, too. Seeing Jennifer's book on the shelf might motivate a renewed commitment to steward our looks for Jesus, but within six months, it's as if we never read it. We are recidivists at heart.

Jennifer calls it the Bible Camp Effect. Are we all susceptible? "Yeah," she told me. "My hand is raised. I have to fight the demons of approval (i.e., love idols) almost every day."[8]

Integration is tough.

I took a student government president and future lawyer on a backpacking trip to North Carolina. Rob was also president of the honors program and social chair of his fraternity while maintaining a full academic course load. This was a young man who lived by his watch. When we arrived at the trailhead, I talked with the group about how this would be a chance to reset our rhythms. We'd sleep when we felt tired and eat when we got hungry. I added that we are so dependent on schedules and artificial light, we forget how to pay attention to those things.

"To help reset those routines," I said, "I'm going to collect anything that tells time, and I'll put it in the van." Rob immediately refused. I couldn't force him, but since he was a pre-law major and I knew what good it could do, I asked for his reasons. We went back and forth for several minutes—the entire group gathered around the two of us—until I thought of a deal.

"All right, Rob. How about this? You give me your watch, and I'll let you look at it once each day, whenever you choose." He closed his eyes for a moment and then handed it to me. Everyone cheered.

Shortly after, I approached Rob and thanked him for showing courage. I promised to uphold my end of the deal, but I also asked him to try what he thought was the impossible: to let his watch go for the next eight days. One day turned into the next and then into the next, and he didn't ask to see it. The topic arose often at first, and then it didn't. He began to experience the freedom of living outside of his hectic, time-based life, and he confessed that he hadn't felt so free in years.

When we returned to campus, I handed back his watch, but he didn't put it on. "I'm not going to wear it for the rest of the semester," he said. "I don't want to be bound by this thing anymore."

I looked him up recently and asked if he remembered that scene. It's been more than fifteen years. Rob said, "I remember both the trip and the watch issue fondly to this day." He told me that he never returned to wearing his watch as religiously as he had before the trip. In fact, he thanked me for taking it. "Whether it's a few hours for a hike in the woods or a summer vacation to the shore, the time I get to unplug, rare though it may be, is a gift I still appreciate."

But what is a guy like that to do when he leads a busy life and when technology is so much more entertaining these days? Good intentions or not, it seems impossible to maintain simple idealism. He confessed as much: "As tightly as I clung to my watch in North Carolina, I feel that my smartphone and Apple Watch have just as strong—if not a stronger—hold on me now. It's largely a function of my job. We're expected to be accessible to clients 24/7, and anyone who isn't doesn't last long."

Would he—*could* he—surrender if we took the trip again next week? Are there spiritual disciplines or practices someone like Rob could employ on a regular basis, like unplugging on the sabbath or during meal times? After all, backpacking trips are only one way to experience growth.

Integration is hard to carry out for a variety of reasons, as these stories reveal and as you and I know from our own lives.[9]

INTEGRATION QUESTIONS

Consider these sample questions about my encounter with Ed, the homeless man. (For tips on how to implement new learning, see "Getting Practical" below.)

Questions I asked myself:

- What is Jesus calling me to do about this insight?

- How does Ed want to be treated?

- How should I respond to the next homeless person I meet?

Questions you could ask me (if not the ones I asked myself):

- You're one of the leaders on this trip. How could you use this encounter to help the participants grow?

- Are there other trips you could sign up for or books that could continue your growth?

GETTING PRACTICAL

All of this makes returning home a critical moment. Your adventure may have felt life changing, but it won't change your life if you resume your routine. Same job, same relationships—that's fine. Just make sure you don't go back to them in the same way. As a friend says, "What you feed grows. What you starve dies." The little (or big) seed given to you while you were away needs proper attention. No matter how epic a journey you take, how many life-stretching miles you travel, or how unimaginably difficult your designed experience turns out to be, lessons can't be left lying around and expected to take root.

> YOUR ADVENTURE MAY HAVE FELT LIFE CHANGING, BUT IT WON'T CHANGE YOUR LIFE IF YOU RESUME YOUR ROUTINE.

T. S. Eliot observed, "We had the experience but missed the meaning." He then went on to say, "And approach to the meaning restores the experience in a different form."[10] I'd like to finish this chapter with seven practical tips for approaching the meaning so that we can return well.

1. Say thanks. Sunshine and ease? Sleet and hardship? Tell God (and anyone else involved) thanks. As we all know, the worst scenarios can produce the best outcomes.

2. See the experience as a passage, not an ending. Recent college grad Makenna Huff turned her five-hundred-mile pilgrimage walk across northern Spain into a senior thesis. She wrote this about El Camino de Santiago: "Walking is not just a form of transportation, ascetic struggle, or endorphin release. To the pilgrim actually experiencing the journey, performing the extended ritual of walking to a holy place creates a sense of deep connectedness to the spaces being passed through, making them sacred places."[11] Like the pilgrim pools in Psalm 84, these sacred places help us "go from strength to strength, till each appears before God in Zion" (v. 7).

3. Tell your story. Unpack what happened. This is one of the more frequent commands in the Old Testament. Don't feel bad if you struggle to find words when people ask, "How was your run/trip/retreat?" because, seriously, how can you answer a generic question like that when your entire perspective got shifted? To help you process, try one of the following:

- Spend an afternoon alone to journal and reflect.[12] I do this near a local cornfield where the traffic is minimal and I can process out loud to myself.

- Meet with a pastor, counselor, or mentor. He or she can help make sense of your reflections.

- Invite a close friend to ask you specific (and hard) questions.

4. Make an Ebenezer. The Israelites captured their experience of God's provision by erecting a pile of stones, one stone for each of the twelve tribes. Over time, Ebenezers serve as waypoints along our faith journeys, marking the route we've traveled. This can be as simple as a defining photo or quote or Bible verse, which can be printed out with a note on the back. For a not-so-wilderness-friendly option, scratch a few words into the beaver dam stick that you brought home. If you finished a marathon, an Ebenezer can signify the moment you most wanted to quit but didn't. If it was a fast, the Ebenezer can be the tear you shed when the fast really cost you. Author Ann Kroeker captured her learning moment with an article called "Seeing the World,"[13] in which she realized for the first time in her life that she was a foreigner. That article was an Ebenezer.

5. Implement a new rule of living. Create this rule *right now*. Only don't try to squeeze it into your life; instead, let it replace a current item that poses a threat. For me, the rule meant consulting my calendar realistically before saying yes to new work opportunities. I made this rule during my sabbatical when my calendar was on hold, and when I returned to work, my stress dropped significantly. For you, it might mean committing to walk every morning or to cancel Netflix.

Whatever it is, make it simple and measurable, like when my wife, Julie, wanted to see if practicing gratitude would make her more grateful. She began with Ann Voskamp's *One Thousand Gifts*, as I mentioned in the introduction, then started a gratitude journal on her thirty-ninth birthday. The goal was a thousand entries in 365 days, and she established a ritual to maintain focus: write a few phrases in a journal she liked with a pen that was attached, while sitting in her favorite chair with a cup of coffee or tea. It was so easy that it became enjoyable, and she stuck with it.

"Did it work?" I asked the other night. "I mean, did you feel more grateful?"

"Yes, I still do."

"I've noticed, you know, but I wondered what you thought. By the way, what ever happened with your journal?"

"I kept going, to 2,224! I had to wean myself off," she said, laughing. "There's always something to be thankful for, even if it's just chicken patties."

6. *Commit encouragement to memory*. "Make every effort to add to your faith goodness; and to goodness, knowledge; and to knowledge, self-control; and to self-control, perseverance; and to perseverance, godliness; and to godliness, mutual affection; and to mutual affection, love. For if you possess these qualities in increasing measure, they will keep you from being ineffective and unproductive in your knowledge of our Lord Jesus Christ" (2 Peter 1:5-8).

7. *Schedule the next adventure*. This is not to encourage you to become an adrenaline junkie, but to encourage deeper maturity. For example, as you plan your next quest, make it about others, not just yourself. When four thousand Sudanese refugees were invited to the United States, tribal elders gave them an others-centered vision: "Dear ones, our people are trying to return Sudan to normal. [You] are going to the US because you are the future of Sudan. They are going to educate you. Get what you're going for, and then come back home."[14] This turns the question from "Why do I need to have this experience?" to "Who needs me to have this experience?"

NAVIGATING VALLEYS

8

*The danger is not lest the soul should doubt
whether there is any bread, but lest, by a lie, it
should persuade itself that it is not hungry.*

SIMONE WEIL

Tonight's local news will contain the usual: a weather report, sports updates, and possibly a cute story about kids decorating pumpkins. Most of the hour, though, will cover stories of brokenness, with the raped, robbed, and guilty appearing in our living rooms in raw form. We'll hear about the latest fraud, kidnapping, drunk driving, poisoning, flood, and protest—the bulk of the carnage reported locally. International and national news aside, this is only one newscast in one city, just the stories our hometown reporters believe will keep us watching.

Zoom in to my street—my block alone, in fact—and you'll find news of an eviction notice, an engagement that just ended, a psychological evaluation, insurance problems, chronic obstructive pulmonary disease, and visits to a treatment facility for anorexia. You'll also hear about the twenty-five-year-old grandson who braved it through two years of chemotherapy and radiation to finally be told he could receive part of his mother's liver. With high hopes, the surgeon cut him open and found more cancer. They didn't have to walk far to tell Mom the whole thing was off. She was in the next room already hooked up to the IV. We live in a fine neighborhood in an award-winning school district with wonderful neighbors, but the grandmother cried on the phone to me about her grandson and now her daughter whose hope has been silenced.

This story didn't make the news. None from my block has.

Multiply the half-dozen localized stories that will air tonight on each of ABC's 238 affiliates across the United States, and you get approximately 1,400 tragedies deemed reportable. Just tonight. I mentioned another half dozen from neighbors within throwing distance of our house. We're talking five hundred linear feet of living space—less than one-tenth of a mile of residential houses. Multiply that by your block and every other block in this country and then by all of the inhabited countries across the planet, and the amount of unwelcomed, unplanned pain going on right now on the globe is crushing. If each of us has only one personal issue, that's over seven billion stories of pain. And many of us carry multiple burdens.

Karl Rahner writes, "In the torment of the insufficiency of everything attainable we come to understand that here, in this life, all symphonies remain unfinished."[1] I appreciate Ronald Rolheiser's response:

> What does it mean to be tormented by the insufficiency of everything attainable? We all experience this daily. This torment is generally an undertow to everyday life: beauty makes us restless when it should give us peace; the love we

experience with others does not fulfill our deep longings; the relationships we have within our families seem too domestic to be fulfilling; our job is inadequate to the dreams we have for ourselves; the place we live seems "small town" in comparison to other places; the ideal we have for our lives habitually crucifies the reality of our lives and makes us too restless to sit peacefully at our own tables, to sleep peacefully in our own beds, and be at ease within our own skins. Our lives seem too small for us, and we are always waiting for something or somebody to come along and change things so that our real lives, as we imagine them, might begin.[2]

These poignant lines jumped from the pages at me near the end of my midlife transition. It lasted two years and was marked by frustration and doubt. Our house had come close to burning down, one of our daughters entered a perplexing time of illness, and I was overwhelmed at work and then contracted Lyme disease, which presented itself as bacterial meningitis and sent me into quarantine for five days. Julie was shutting down because of it all happening simultaneously.

People have more serious issues, I know. But these were our issues—my issues—and they weighed on us. We were in "torment of the insufficiency of everything attainable," as Rahner so succinctly put it, and no prayer we prayed, no solutions we applied, freed us.

Looking back, I see that these challenges were affiliated with a project I had taken on—a series of audio stories about a three-year period in my teenage years. What did my fourteen-year-old self have to do with my forty-year-old self? A lot, it turns out, when you haven't resolved "dad issues." I had enjoyed a Peter Pan–like relationship with my father as a boy, but it worsened over time. Aggravations became blowups, which turned into divisions and regret.

He died before we could repair much of what had been damaged, leaving me with unfinished business and haunting my way forward. I couldn't shake him. Oddly, the events in my midlife brought his haunting to a climax.

Like most unplanned experiences, these events came like a thief in the night. They didn't come as intentional exercises to stretch my faith in the God I praised for being full of blessings. God was absent regarding the solutions I thought we needed, which meant I was a prime candidate for quick fixes. Some-

GOD WAS ABSENT REGARDING THE SOLUTIONS I THOUGHT WE NEEDED, WHICH MEANT I WAS A PRIME CANDIDATE FOR QUICK FIXES.

times I gave in; sometimes I abstained. It's hard to show "love, joy, peace, forbearance, kindness, goodness, faithfulness, gentleness, and self-control" (Galatians 5:22-23) when you hurt. These gifts are other-oriented.

Still, God was good. With space between then and now, how can I say that he was not? Why, for instance, did our toughest year as a family coincide with the toughest internal work for me? I never intended to confront my father-son issues the year we felt like we were drowning. Nor did I intend to work out my issues through audio recordings about adventures in a faraway state twenty-five years ago. The stories weren't even about my dad. Yet they were enough about him and about me and about me now in his old shoes as an adult that the parallel events contributed to resolving aspects of my own life's symphony. The stories invited me to see what I could not have seen otherwise.

Here is what I can share about that difficult year, including reasons I've been able to carry the lessons forward to other hard times.

First, I continued practicing the habits I had always practiced—those things you do when life is going well. I went to church when I didn't want to. I prayed when I didn't know if it mattered. I picked up our kids when it was cold or raining and I wanted to stare at the floor instead. I labored at my job when dragging myself out of bed was the least desirable thing to do. I did none of these right actions with stellar success, but I tried because I knew that shutting down would lead to nowhere useful.

Second, I kept telling stories. *A Beautiful Trench It Was: Audio Vignettes of a Boy* (abeautifultrenchitwas.com) provided focus—or distraction, I'm not sure which. I'd tell one story, with the plan to tell another the next week, and then another.

I imagined it would be easy—just get the words out and do it. But it came together differently than that. Each story took more from me than expected and yet somehow fed me more than expected. The days between recordings presented the most challenge because, as I'd discover, I was working through current problems with their assistance. As they proceeded week after week, I kept running into current issues in surprisingly related ways—simply grownup versions. Some tales were full of labor and emotion (you can hear it in my voice, which friends and family said didn't sound like me), while others came with delight. Some tales involved how I handled a problem with my parents. Same with 2013, only reversed, as I was now the parent. And so on. It took nine months to get them all out.

(And even then, I was not done. The emotional toll the year had taken and the void I felt after finishing the project caused me to spiral further downward. In one telling moment, during a work-related phone call with my friend and then managing editor, Deidra, I broke. For a solid hour, I cried while she listened and my wife held me. *What was happening?* By January 2014, I was watching eight hours of Netflix every evening and sleeping on the couch—maddened by requests, obligations, and the slightest noises. I wanted to be alone.)

Third, I got off the couch. Specifically, I got dressed one morning that same bleak January when the wind chill was negative four, and

I drove to a parking area near the Appalachian Trail. There was too much snow for anyone else to be there, so I went for a walk. The biting cold squeezed my lungs. The popping ice filled my ears as each boot broke through the crust into the soft powder below. The bright sun lit up the white earth and made my eyes tear. Knees and ankles and quadriceps fired signals to my brain for oxygen and balance. I began to sweat. I removed layers of clothing, even as my beard and moustache froze. For the first time in months, life entered my bones.

It would take another year—including a three-month sabbatical, continued meetings with a pastor, and a short-term antidepressant to take off the sharpest edge—before I would feel free. But that walk was a turning point. It soon became a run and then a 5k, soccer, working in the yard, playing with the kids. I was back. Until then, however, Jesus had work to do, and there was nothing I could do to stop him. Rolheiser continues,

> To accept that we cannot have the full symphony gives us permission to have a bad day, a lonely season, a life that somehow never fully gets free of tension and restlessness. It gives us permission as well not to be too hard on ourselves and, more importantly, it tells us to stop putting unfair pressure on our spouses, families, friends, vacations, and jobs to give us something that they cannot give—namely, happiness without a shadow, the full symphony. We move beyond the cancer of frustration and restlessness by precisely accepting that here, in this life, there is no finished symphony.[3]

The psalmist tells of a man who is "like a tree planted by streams of water, which yields its fruit in season and whose leaf does not wither" (Psalm 1:3). That same man is one who faces all manner of trials. Those trials come to both the wise and the foolish (Matthew 7:24-27), implying that no one can hide from pain. The roots make a difference in how we are sustained. The foundation makes a difference in how the storm affects us. I will probably go through harder times, and I may not fare as well. What is there for me to do in the meantime? The simple things, really, like telling stories about God showing up when I was fourteen and about going for a walk when it's so cold my breath turned to crystals.

SELF-DENIAL

We are anesthesiologists by nature, which is why self-denial is central in our progression toward maturity. Self-denial forces us to deal with difficulty, not run from it like I wanted to do during my midlife transition. Succumbing has no training value. It does not make us more resilient or better prepared for anything that shows up unannounced. I've heard it said that maturity stops when addiction begins, which makes sense: coping mechanisms offer an alternative to working through difficulty. Instead, we should be like Jacob, who refused to end his struggle with the man of God until he received a blessing (Genesis 32:22-26). Denying ourselves of workarounds produces a perseverance that makes us "mature and complete, not lacking anything" (James 1:4).

It's bad enough to suffer, but then Jesus sees me eyeing up a thing I know would make me feel better, and says, "Whoever wants to be my disciple must deny themselves and take up their cross and follow me" (Matthew 16:24). To be fair, denying ourselves is not a call to extreme asceticism. Jesus doesn't mind a trip to Disney World or a nap in the hammock. Gnosticism, the belief that only the spiritual realm has value, wasn't his thing. It's just that self-denial often feels like this: no fun. In truth, self-denial is the practice of refusing anything that stands in place of God's provision, whether or not he provides in that moment.

I'm reminded of Jen from chapter one, the woman who was afraid to stop the backpacking group when low sugar took its toll.

In that moment, she was wrestling with two pains in her life: a headache and fear. The only viable fix she saw was one that ignored them both: not stopping the group. Addressing the headache felt too risky since stopping for M&M's would expose her as weak, and addressing insecurity felt too scary.

We're discussing self-denial here, which is often a painful act. Was Jen's pain—either one—the kind we should aim for? No. Her headache was not a thing to make her stronger, but to be quelled, and Jehovah Jireh, God our Provider (via farmers and the Mars candy company) had provided M&M's to rebalance her glucose level. That's a good thing. But the pain of the fear of being unloved, if she were exposed, was too big, and its balm too out of reach, to give her hope. The new heaven and new earth often seem similar—far away and unattainable. By ignoring both pains and pressing on, Jen could protect herself. She'd have to live with the unfortunate headache, but she'd be safe from deeper concerns.

This, in my opinion, makes Jesus' command the hardest one of all. Don't murder, don't steal—I can abide by those. But deny myself of the tiny fragments that could ease the struggle? Maybe for you it's shopping or eating. Maybe it's masturbation or bragging. Or the "white lies" of coping. Mere venial sins, mild infractions. And yet they do so much for us—for me—in the moment. Still, Jesus says no. *I have something better for you, but it's on the other side of what causes pain right now.*

It helps, in a way, that he practiced what he preached. That famous line about denying the self came from an exchange with his closest friend. Jesus was telling the disciples about future troubles and preparing them for his death when Peter cried, "Never, Lord! . . . This shall never happen to you!" (Matthew 16:22).

For centuries, the people had waited for the Messiah to rebuild their kingdom. They desired freedom, and Jesus knew it. The devil's early interactions with Jesus in the desert came littered with rulership elements. Here was a gifted man with prophecies attached to his birth and paternal *and* maternal ancestry to the great kings of Israel. His ability to draw enormous crowds would prove him to be highly influential. Jesus was the prime candidate to respond to the problem, which made the content of his temptations a serious matter.

I used to read the desert account in Matthew 4 like my first invitation to join Amway. Malcolm had been the pot smoker on our high school bus. One day, a few years after graduation, I bumped into him, and he invited me to lunch. At the restaurant, his out-of-character suit and stack of picture albums (yes, albums) caught me off guard. We ordered sandwiches, and he asked, "Have you ever thought about what you want to accomplish, Sam? Wouldn't it be great to be rich and spend your days traveling?" Then he showed me picture after picture of RVs in various locations across the United States. I was twenty-two and said no.

It's easy to imagine Jesus in the desert as if he were on a mildly challenging retreat, accompanied by a questionable salesman with irrelevant wares. The Savior-to-be responds like I did to Malcolm and walks away victoriously. But this tame picture denies the humanity of Christ. It denies that "he himself suffered when he was tempted" (Hebrews 2:18) and diminishes him "who has been tempted in every way, just as we are" (4:15).

Peter's rebuke tapped into this old temptation. It had savor to it. Jesus didn't walk away effortlessly but desperately, like when you're cornered. "Get behind me, Satan! You are a stumbling block to me" (Matthew 16:23). It wasn't Peter he silenced but the very real offer to apply his own remedy. The words that followed about denial and taking up the cross supported what Jesus himself had just accomplished in the face of temptation. I hear Leslie Fiedler's ruminations on the French philosopher Simone Weil:

Here below we must be content to be . . . hungry; indeed, we must *welcome* hunger, for it is the sole proof we have of the reality of God, who is the only sustenance that can satisfy us, but one which is "absent" in the created world. "The danger is not lest the soul should doubt whether there is any bread [God], but lest, by a lie, it should persuade itself that it is not hungry."[4]

Jen needed to stop the group even if they thought poorly of her for it. Her hunger was for love, but she didn't know if she'd find it in that moment, so she refused the risk altogether. Weil recognized the pain in waiting and still says it is best, because in the risk we come closest to Jesus. He is the one who proved that we should take it. Difficult words.

PHOTURIS AND OTHER APPROXIMATIONS

Why is refusing so difficult? Because hunger confounds our ability to distinguish real from imitation. Here's an example in the illustration "The lure of the predatory *Photuris* female."

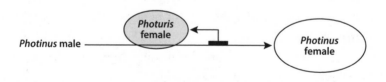

The lure of the predatory *Photuris* female

The predatory female firefly from the genus *Photuris* lures unsuspecting males of the genus *Photinus* by mimicking the light of the *Photinus* female. The predator's flashing pattern is not exactly like the genuine, but the scientifically recorded difference between the two is so slight and the male's natural desire so strong for *Photinus* that *Photuris* fools him. In other words, she taps into the normative draw of the *Photinus* female to gain the male's attention.

The predator has nothing of her own to offer. Even if she did, it wouldn't be effective, because the male is hardwired with a "hunger" for a specific lighting pattern. So the predator must resort to borrowing actual, enticing elements of the good lighting pattern, resulting in something like what's shown in the illustration.

Photuris obviously functions as an idol. The small black box represents her extraction work, like my uncle tapping into his neighbor's line to get cable television. And there is a consequence to the male's idolatry: *Photuris* eats him. Not all of our refusals to wait turn out like this, fortunately. If we replace the labels from *Photuris* to something else—pick a poison in your own life—the illustration "The lure of an idol" shows how we fall for the same scheme.

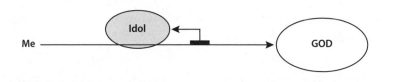

The lure of an idol

The straight arrow now represents the draw of God's love—that clear invitation toward Home that contains everything we are intended to hunger for: full satisfaction, perfect peace, unconditional acceptance, fair justice, sweet intimacy—every one a beautiful shape of God's love. Just like the *Photinus* male, we are hardwired for a healthy satisfaction. But as Paul reminds us in 1 Corinthians 13:12, we only "know in part."

The adventure program Outward Bound began because sailors were struggling to survive after shipwrecks and Nazi submarine attacks. Lawrence Holt, a steamship company president, made a critical observation when he noticed that most of the sailors who died were young and healthy. Who survived? Their older, weaker counterparts. It's a surprise *anyone* passed through such experiences, considering the traumatic conditions. With land miles away, especially at night and in cold that could kill in minutes, who could last?

The older sailors had experience. They had tougher skin. They had learned about perseverance and how to deny themselves of an easier solution: the option to slip beneath the waves. "C'mon, you know what you want," *Photuris* whispers seductively to their tired arms and hearts. But the mental toughness gained along the way helped them endure.[5]

The blessing goes to those who are willing to pay more for it. And veteran sailors were willing to pay more. This clear-cut distinction regarding maturity led experiential educator Kurt Hahn to begin training Holt's sailors. Today, Outward Bound exists in thirty-three countries and serves 250,000 participants each year (see outwardbound.net).

If we believe that God "is the only sustenance that can satisfy us," as Fiedler wrote, then it is foolishness, or maybe laziness, that tricks us into putting faith in idols instead. The fragments of pleasure in gossip or smoking or bragging or revenge cannot sustain us. We know it makes no sense, but some pleasure is better than no pleasure, and no pain is better than some pain. Toughness

THE FRAGMENTS OF PLEASURE IN GOSSIP OR SMOKING OR BRAGGING OR REVENGE CANNOT SUSTAIN US.

gained by welcoming hunger—whether by force or by design—provides a new kind of patience. It keeps us from sinking beneath the waves before we actually run out of strength.

FAMILIARITY WITH SOLUTIONS

Ironically, pursuing *unhealthy* options is related to our pursuit of *healthy* options. We rest from the flu and mourn the loss of a relative. We add raincoats to a stormy day and compression socks to relieve varicose veins. In countless ways, we maneuver our lives toward greater ease—a perfectly normal endeavor. Like the student leaders I sent into the brush at Dolly Sods, lost people will do everything possible to relieve the anxiety of feeling lost. This is good.

But coping becomes complicated as judgment declines. According to the search-planning book *Analysis of Lost Person Behavior*, "When direction of travel was examined, it was found to be influenced by terrain, as well as denseness and type of vegetation. . . . Persons continually sought paths of least resistance, regardless of direction. This was also true of alternative drainages. If three alternatives were available, the final selection was made on 'looks.'"[6]

There's the subtle shift. The normal pursuit of resolution—the good desire to be found—moves from clearheadedness to confusion as the patience required to wait turns into fear and desperation. This is when the paths of least resistance look so appealing. We need hunger to unsettle us, or we become like the child who closes his eyes and believes the bad guys have disappeared. Paul knew that God alone satisfies:

> We know that "An idol is nothing at all in the world" and that "There is no God but one." For even if there are so-called gods, whether in heaven or on earth (as indeed there are many "gods" and many "lords"), yet for us there is but one God, the Father, from whom all things came and for whom we live; and there is but one Lord, Jesus Christ, through whom all things came and through whom we live. (1 Corinthians 8:4-6)

What is drawing me? Which one is Photinus *and which is* Photuris? *What is here that I really want?* Helen Cepero, the author of

Christ-Shaped Character, says, "To actually name what we want, our true desire, might well mean facing hurt and pain. It will almost certainly require us to listen to ourselves at a deep level."[7] By paying attention in this way—listening to our hunger and even sitting with it for a time because we care about satisfying it correctly—we gain a valuable tool. We discover what lies beneath the hunger, effectively clarifying the Object of our hope and broadening our capacity for self-denial.

Cepero also gives us permission to be optimistic in these hunger moments: "It is not about settling for less than we hoped; it is about longing for More—living and praying our way through all the ways we may have settled until we see the truth."[8] This leads to a bold surrender to Jesus the Savior and Craftsman, "who began a good work in you [and] will carry it on to completion" (Philippians 1:6). The Savior rescues us; the Craftsman improves us. In one role, he offers the deepest balm for our pain; in the other, he teaches us that he alone is the source.

PRACTICING TO WAIT

Here is the tough truth: when you return from a designed experience, however formative it may have been, you've still got the same creepy neighbor and the same credit card bill. You still have a chemotherapy appointment tomorrow. Nothing can change that fact, because the rest of life's experiences—the undesigned, unplanned ones—are pushing and pulling outside of your control. Lice come home from school with the kids whether you like it or not. And what can prepare you for Dad cheating on Mom? Hardship may promise to shape our lives positively, but rarely can we see that until we're further down the road. Right now that kick-starting feels more like being kicked.

And being kicked hurts. It is the presence of pain and the absence of relief. It is also the absence of control and, if times are tough enough, what appears to be the absence of God. Then just at that point when we think we've had enough, a graver challenge presents itself: Jesus tells us to set aside the balms we use to console ourselves and wait for relief. How do we handle this hunger like men and women marked by faith, hope, and love?

One of the most effective means of reorienting our relationship with hunger is to sit with it. Sit with it and ask what it wants. Food hunger has an obvious (and legitimate) solution. Revenge hunger does not. Shopping hunger does not. These are often distorted by emotion or pain, and so we sit until we are able to see them as a longing to have what God promises. This doesn't alleviate the pain, but it makes it more bearable as recognition begins to dismantle the belief that true fulfillment is available now.

In the meantime, shortcuts seem to increase in availability and in appeal. Exile hangs on like dead weight, and idols make it easier to bear. Their seduction is like the audience member who told me, "I know idols aren't the real deal, but they're predictable and available. I'll settle for *Photuris* a hundred times before having to wait even once for the genuine. It's just easier." Oh, man, do you hear that?

The less we sit, the more our behavior goes from bad to worse as hunger compounds with the doubt that God will deliver us. In this, we are no different today than ancient peoples who constantly settled for alternatives, because we too hear, "They will be my people, and I will be their God" (Jeremiah 32:38).

Yet God has not shown up as we wish. We want the renewal of all things, but our frail will leads us to continue crying out for substitute leaders to take us back to Egypt. "Our hearts are restless till they find rest in thee," St. Augustine proclaimed. The harder the challenge or the more traumatic the event, the more difficult self-denial becomes. What a predicament we are in! And yet sit we must.

Rolheiser offers comfort and a word of counsel toward this end: "To be tormented by complexity and restlessness is to be human. To make our peace with that is to come to peace, and we are mature to the degree that our own restlessness is no longer the center of our lives."[9] Friend, this is what we want. So rest in the promises of God and watch your hunger turn to hope, however long it takes, for "hope is not based on something that will happen after our sufferings are over, but on the real presence of God's healing Spirit in the midst of these sufferings."[10]

Just don't do it alone. In chapter nine, we'll honor the role of fellow disciples who serve as trailblazers committed to facing forward, as truth tellers calling us to press on, and as recipients of our own growing maturity.

GETTING

9

UNSTUCK TOGETHER

Three times this week, I stayed up too late. Three times. It's not like this is anything new in my life—I've been a night owl for years. When Julie and I took the Automated Morningness-Eveningness Questionnaire,[1] I scored in the "definite evening" range—that is, night owl. I often catch a second wind around 10 p.m. and can go strong until the wee hours.

But Lent has hardly passed, and my commitment to turning out the lights at eleven is already dimming. I'm not ready for this. I liked what I saw over the past forty days. I was more consistent, more disciplined, more productive. I was even, somehow, more focused, which is odd because I quit an ADD medicine in February—a decision that left me painfully tired. My daughter found me one afternoon sitting up, head against the wall, hands at rest on the keyboard, out cold. I'm not a napper, so we both got a laugh.

What does this have to do with pursuing maturity together? As a steward of my body, I've wondered for several years what impact additional (and regular) sleep could have on me. I have been so notoriously inconsistent with bedtimes and wake times that the occasional desperate attempt to catch up by binge sleeping only leaves me cranky. Cutting the ADD med forced my hand. In those first few days prior to Ash Wednesday, I couldn't wait to go to bed. It was then that I committed to testing sleep for real.

Jesus had plenty of advice to give in his Sermon on the Mount, and I supposed a good many of the convictions I'd get when hearing it were due to sleeplessness. This led me to ask, *Would faith increase if I had a fuller tank of patience? Would I gain hope by having better stamina? Would sufficient rest improve my capacity to love?*

Signs indicated yes to all three. Forty days was too short to say for certain, which is why I was not ready for it to end. As I said, I liked what I saw. For one, it was disrupting a pattern I had carried on for years:

- Stay up late. (Who doesn't like Jimmy Fallon?)
- Finally turn off the TV or woodworking shop light, depending on the day.
- Suddenly get smacked by how tired I feel and (if due to TV) how much time I had wasted.
- Fall asleep immediately.
- Respond to two morning alarms with the weight of lead and the mobility of stiff molasses.
- Curse my night-owl self for ignoring how painful waking up would be.
- Repeat the cycle the next evening as if it had never happened before.

Seriously, when the cycle began again the following evening, I wouldn't feel tired. I'd have no recollection of my insightful morning self. Mr. Hyde did not know Dr. Jekyll. *I* knew the two existed; they did not. This Lenten fast was a way to lock them in the same room and have them duke it out.

And duke it out they did. Nearly every night brought pain: "Whyyy do I have to go to bed right now? I am *not* tired."

And Julie would say, "Shhh. C'mon, you'll appreciate the decision in the morning."

Even in the final week of Lent, I struggled to make that right decision. I would do it, but I didn't want to. Then Jesus arose on Easter morning, and I was free again to do what I wanted. Surprisingly, I wanted to go to bed at eleven. Huh? Something seemed to be taking hold.

Without Julie's help, I'm sure I would have slouched. After all, it was a self-made goal that I didn't really want to keep and that (at least at night) I couldn't see the reason for keeping. Now I could see a reason.

So how is it possible to witness positive results, discover a good solution leading to those results, and then threaten that good by separating Night Owl Sam from Morning Sam before the two could finish working things out? I don't know. But with three late-night infractions just this week, it's clear that I still need help.

Years ago, I found this quote by author Larry Crabb taped to a professor's door:

> One of the most liberating discoveries that I've made is that I don't really have an inadequacy complex. . . . I really am inadequate. My sense of inadequacy is not a disorder that needs therapy. It's not a deficiency that needs correction by further training. It's something that must be embraced as an opportunity to depend on God in ways that I never have before.

Well-designed experiences, even simple diagnostic ones like the spiritual discipline of getting more sleep, can be powerful. But our lack of adequacy and our self-insufficiency get us stuck again. In my case, I'm liable to get restuck before I'm fully unstuck. The promise of transformation has to compete with old norms, old likes, and (depending on the situation) maybe even old friends who don't make room for our new ways. As I said in the introduction, our (my) typical patterns are so much like New Year's resolutions that meaningful moments come and go like so many prophetic invitations: convicting and short-lived. Honest acceptance of this fact reveals the need for subsequent and repeated messages. How else will we grow in faith, hope, and love, if not by persistent prodding? We need constant reminders.

> **HOW ELSE WILL WE GROW IN FAITH, HOPE, AND LOVE, IF NOT BY PERSISTENT PRODDING? WE NEED CONSTANT REMINDERS.**

Those reminders come best from the people who travel with us. If Julie proved to be a necessary encouragement during Lent, I may need to ask for her assistance after Lent as well. She has no power of her own to cure me, but in God's beneficence, she has been a gift that helps me get stuck less often and less seriously. That's not all, of course. She needs my help, too. For this reason, we receive the truth from each other. We are reminded by the other of what God has done, and we return the favor. This maturity—pursued together—weakens the stuck cycle because the whole is greater than the sum of its parts. This is the body of Christ (1 Corinthians 12:14), and it works in marriage, in neighborhoods, in churches, in families, in boardrooms— wherever two or more are gathered in his name.

ONE HUMAN IS NO HUMAN

A professor assigned us with defending the statement that "one human is no human." He wanted a six- to eight-page response. I had trouble understanding the statement at all—was it a trick question, perhaps a riddle?

I began by studying the Trinity and discovered a possible angle while reading about the giving and receiving between the Father, Son, and Holy Spirit. Richard Gula wrote, "God in whose image we are made is a community of persons radically equal to each other while absolutely mutual in self-giving and receiving."[2] I wondered, *Would independence practiced by any of the three persons of God render God unGod? Could we say that "one part of God is not God"?* Had Jesus made a decision at any point to take his own path, the Trinity would have been theologically undone.

Continuing the research, I thought about babies and toddlers who can't give as much as they receive, despite the joy they give their parents. In those early years, they need, need, need. They have no solid grasp of any subject area. Instead, they soak up, receiving the environment with all of its colors, shapes, textures, sounds, and smells. They form associations, discover moral lines, test boundaries. They discover what superhero capes can and cannot do.[3] But they don't know enough yet to make it alone. They survive because of community. And I thought, *One child is no family.*

After a few skinned knees, the child's feet become surer. Her confidence grows as she acquires something worth passing along. Here she moves from receiver to receiver-giver. In preschool, she's told to "Find a buddy." That collaborative pairing later becomes "Pick a study partner," and "Get with your project team." In sixth grade, our girls came home with writing assignments that had been peer edited. Their own edits had gone home with classmates.

Instruction shown becomes instruction shared. (This is often when we begin toying with our future: *when I grow up, I want to help people because I'm learning that I'm good at solving problems,* or *I'm good at getting my friends to do fun things.*) In this stage, we might discover we're better with big-picture outlines than final details or that a team functions best when we contribute our individual gifts. And I thought, *One student is no team.*

We grow in our giving as we apply to be geometry tutors or to show new hires how to make French fries. We initiate college clubs and then become grad assistants, mothers, and physicians. We now guide and give. But we play these roles only because there are students to guide and give to. Maturity implies learning; and learning implies pupils. The most learned scholar must continue to be taught. Gula wrote, "The trinitarian vision sees that no one exists by oneself, but only in relationship to others. To be is to be in relationship. The individual and the community coexist. Humanity and relatedness are proportional so that the deeper one participates in relationships, the more human one becomes."[4]

The key is to remain a student capable of receiving while also becoming a teacher competent at giving. This mutual receiving and giving binds us interdependently. It's true that one human is no human. If we get this wrong, we won't get discipleship right.

Below is a selection of examples demonstrating the role of community in the development of maturity.

RECEIVING AND GIVING

Through navigation. The Barkley Marathon is a body-thumping, will-testing, 100-mile pain of a race. Competitors don't even know when the race will begin. Once it does, they have sixty hours to complete five laps, each lap nearly the length of a marathon and covering twelve thousand feet of elevation change. Since its inception in 1986, only fifteen runners have completed all five laps. Most runners drop out during the first lap.

When Jared Campbell entered his initial Barkley in 2012, he ran with Brett Maune until the end of lap four, when Maune pulled ahead to become the first two-time finisher. But Campbell didn't mind losing that time. He knew how important it was to have a teacher showing him the way. He said afterward, when he shook Maune's hand in gratitude, "I would've been lost without this guy. Seriously, thanks, man."[5]

When Campbell returned for a third time in 2016, he went as a teacher. By then, like Maune, he also had completed that beast two times. He was making a name for himself, yet he chose a mature approach. "It was fun to flip the switch," he said, "and give back."[6] But he could do so only because he had been an attentive student.

Navigating countless miles of unmarked trails during the day and through the night and with hardly any sleep demands that you pay attention. As the race host, Gary Cantrell, said, "You can make a tiny mistake and make up for it. But mostly, if you screw up something, you're dead out there on the course."[7]

Similarly, under God's care, Moses led the people from Egypt as a teacher and guide. But he also needed someone with technical skills to guide him. That someone was Hobab, Moses' brother-in-law. According to Numbers 10:31, Moses recruited Hobab, saying, "Please do not leave us. You know where we should camp in the wilderness, and you can be our eyes."

Instruction is perhaps the most common way we receive as students, and it starts early, as Robert Fulghum famously claimed in *All I Really Need to Know I Learned in Kindergarten* (Ballantine, 2004). From parents telling us to look both ways to HR directors acclimating us to new jobs, we move ahead together, thanks to people showing us how.

Through service. Chris and his wife raise kids and host backyard barbecues like most of their friends. Chris also serves as the executive director of PULSE, a disruptive experience that helps "talented university graduates to partner with Pittsburgh nonprofits for a year of service and leadership."[8] Why does a guy with a seemingly normal routine choose to upend life for others? Because he knows the potential impact of disruption on our walk with Jesus, and he loves how that happens in community.

By the end of his college years, Chris and three friends had already flown to Honduras several times for a potable water project. Then an unexpected call inspired them to raise the stakes. Here was the prompt from an acquaintance: "We have an old VW camper bus that's been parked in the yard for years. It doesn't run, but if you can move it, you can have it."

The guys lived a thousand miles south in California and wondered what to do. "We could drive it to Patagonia," one joked. It was too far-fetched, but the idea got them thinking about Central America. "Why not return to Honduras? If we can fix the van, we could continue our previous work there."

Using a repair manual, the four spent a month dismantling and rebuilding the van's engine. They had no experience; they just followed directions. When it was ready, they began the eight-thousand-mile round-trip journey across California, Mexico, and Guatemala to a remote village of the indigenous Pech tribe in northern Honduras.

An experience of this nature and length (three months) creates space for many surprises. The biggest was Hurricane Mitch, which showed up after they arrived. It killed seven thousand Hondurans, destroyed more than 70 percent of the bridges and secondary roads, and according to Honduras's president at the time, removed fifty years of economic development.[9] What Chris and his friends had planned was remarkable enough, but all that?

"One night around two," Chris told me, "someone banged on the window and yelled, 'Wake up! Your van is washing away!'" They forded swollen rivers by homemade canoe and received food and supplies from US helicopters. They joined Red Cross relief efforts. Once a truck full of men with machine guns approached them. "We thought we were done for until we realized it was a police patrol offering to help with our flat tire."

What amazing exposure to decision making, leadership development, and comradery (and risk)! Here's what they had in place: a commitment to an extended trip (time) together in close quarters (shape) without the option of removing themselves (cost) and with an aim to serve (purpose) in a distant country (location). From chapter three, those are the essential five. Chris said to me, "I'm not a big wilderness guy, but the components between what you do in the woods and what we did on that trip are similar, aren't they?" I agreed and he continued. "We had a plan, but it didn't end up like we predicted. As difficult as it was, we embraced the detours as opportunities for growth in Christ, not as obstacles to avoid." They literally got unstuck together.

Through encouragement. I asked Jennifer Dukes Lee about her book *Love Idol* and whether her readers slip back into old patterns as quickly and as often as the rest of us. She affirmed that some do, but added, "If I thought that all my books ever did was offer some kind of Bible camp effect, I doubt I'd write another. Because the truth is, [*Love Idol*] has made a difference. I have heard from women who gave up eating disorders, another who gave up on a retail addiction. I have heard from women who were able to let go of their need for the approval they never got from their dads."[10]

The writer of Hebrews reminds us, "Therefore, since we are surrounded by such a great cloud of witnesses, let us throw off everything that hinders and the sin that so easily entangles. And let us run with perseverance the race marked out for us. . . . Consider [Jesus] who endured such opposition from sinners, so that you will not grow weary and lose heart" (12:1, 3). Encouragement helps readers "run with perseverance," and Jennifer is encouraged in return.

Helen Cepero uses the language of "blessing." It begins as a "look"—that special way a person who loves you sees the best in you. It is the way her pastor knew "that God could see the more that I might be."[11] The look must be received, of course, as one person is no person. As we learn to receive these blessings, we begin to believe new truths about ourselves; however, they are not new, for "God is not making things up for us or reinventing us from nothing when he blesses us. Rather, the light of Christ reveals the possibility of Christlikeness in each of us." God uses his people to help us discover what is already there but hidden.

When a blessing is received and recognized, the fear-filled find courage, the despairing can feel hope, and the timid are able to name their desires. It changes even how we see difficult and painful events in our lives. As a twelve-year-old I would never have chosen to be in that hospital bed. Yet if I had not been in that bed, I would have missed out on the blessing that transformed my life.[12]

It's amazing how it works, isn't it? We see blind spots because of others' vision, and we learn to care because of others' compassion. Is it possible that any movement we've experienced toward maturity was made without the community God placed us in? Even this next example about fire demonstrates this special form of provision.

Through close calls. I've enjoyed playing with fire since I was old enough to know how. I'd throw light bulbs and aerosol cans in the burn pile at Grandpa's house and stand behind the locust tree until they got hot. Light bulbs made a satisfying pop, but the cans shot like little cannons, and I never knew where they would go. I took chances, but every once in a while a close call would sober me, like the time Matt and his friends disappeared in a ball of flames.

We were in the woods, looking for something to do with gunpowder and gasoline. (I did say I took chances.) It had rained significantly earlier in the day, which meant everything was wet. We found a large stump and poured the powder beside it. Then we dowsed the base of the stump with the gasoline—just poured it on. Matt took the matches from his pocket, and I jetted for the nearest tree. I had blown enough cans to have at least some caution.

He lit one and threw it from several feet away. Nothing. I was laughing in that "Oh man, this is fun" kind of way while also yelling for him to be careful. He tried again. Nothing. The other two approached to assist. "Why won't it light?" one of them asked. Now all three were hunched beside the stump, practically leaning on it.

From my vantage point, not only was I able to encourage them to try again, but I had a perfect side view of the scene: tree stump on right, boys facing stump on left.

Another flick and suddenly they were gone. In one whoosh, the flame exploded from the stump and swallowed them whole. Like all good magicians, they reappeared, though not unscathed and smiling like performers on *Penn & Teller: Fool Us.* They were singed and beating themselves frantically. They ran in panic at first and then came to where I stood—to where I was bent over laughing hysterically. All four of us clamored over each other about what just happened. Matt had no eyebrows, the front of his cowlick had curled up short from the heat, and what small progress had been made toward facial hair had vanished. The best part was that his friend had peed himself entirely—jeans soaked down to the knees. We laughed even harder. When the fun passed, I noted, in a rather serious way, to pay fire its due respect.

Today I teach others how to build and manage safe fires. How much of my instruction came from close calls like that one?

***Through* paideia.** When Emma turned five, we adopted a reflective style of discipline because it fit her personality type. One afternoon, I heard her yell, "Daddy! Daaaddyyy! Hurry!" I ran into the room to see that Alice had thrown up all over the two of them and the living-room floor.

"What happened?!" I asked, trying to stay calm. Alice hadn't been sick a minute before.

"I don't know. She was sitting on my lap, and then she threw up."

"Were your arms around her waist?"

"Yes."

"Did you squeeze her?"

"A little?"

I needed more information. "Did you squeeze her or did you *squeeeze* her?"

REAL RESULTS

Between 1995 and 2012, XD hosted fifteen experiences called Leadership and Discipleship in the Wilderness, each one lasting forty days.[13] In 2015, Alexis Zanias of Montreat College tracked down the participants to see what impact those trips had made, if any. Using standardized techniques for gathering and analyzing data, this is what she found:

- Community and challenge are the most significant aspects in this long-term wilderness expedition. (83 percent reported community as most significant.)

- Identity (self-discovery) is the clearest result.

- The natural environment intensifies growth.

- Growth is seen in relationships.

- Transfer of learning is helped through discipleship.

Not everyone can get away for forty days. Fewer people would choose to spend those forty days in the wilderness. But look at the role community played. The impact of an experience—especially one that meets the design criteria in appendix B—is aided by the people who walk through it with us.

"I *squeeezed* her."

I got them both cleaned up, and since Emma was five, I sat her on the bottom step for five minutes while I finished the floor. When the time ended, I joined her and said, "It's okay, sweetie. Alice will be fine." Emma appeared remorseful, and I asked, "What have you learned from this?"

She said, "The next time I squeeze my sister, I better get out of the way!"

It wasn't exactly what I wanted to hear, but it was a start. Discipline, from the Greek *paideia*, is meant to adjust our behavior through education. It isn't punishment as much as it is instruction. Solomon equated discipline with love:

> My son, do not despise the LORD's discipline,
> and do not resent his rebuke,
> because the LORD disciplines those he loves,
> as a father the son he delights in. (Proverbs 3:11-12)

Quoting the same passage, the writer of Hebrews said, "Do not lose heart when he rebukes you" (12:5). I don't want my kids to lose heart when I discipline them (though I know I've done it), which is why I refrained in that moment from giving Emma another time-out to get a better answer.

She is now fifteen, and we have gained extensively from each other in this regard. That's how it works between parents and kids: both parties are subject to consequences for our actions, and though parents do most of the *paideia* work, we learn to be recipients of it as well. The old time-out step has been replaced by conversation, confession, and navigating a way forward as a family.

Through invitation. Growth is pursued together, which brings me back to Allie and her awful bus ride in the Andes. As a facilitator by trade, I am often asked to lead a group through an experience. Rarely do I know the participants who sign up beforehand, and rarely is it possible to maintain a relationship with them afterward. For this reason, especially for longer and more intensive experiences, my colleagues and I make it a practice to connect with someone who *can* maintain those relationships.

Before heading to Peru, I met with Allie's campus minister, Katherine, who told me about her and why she thought our trip would be good for her. After the trip, we talked again, this time about what I saw. I shared highlights as well as thoughts about where Allie might benefit next. I continue to connect with Allie when I can, but my specific role in her life ended when Katherine resumed influence. She pursued Allie, invested in her, mentored her, and encouraged her around this new growth. And as Allie responded, others got involved.

For example, a fellow trip member, Dani, called her regularly. And a new roommate, Kristin, became, as Allie described, "a beautiful part of my faith journey, because she invited me into a healthy college lifestyle." The sparks that appeared on that bus were being fanned into flame. Allie was even convinced to sign up for two additional extended experiences, one of them with Dani and the other a summer-long leadership intensive called the Ocean City Beach Project.[14]

The design work behind that Peru trip served as just one piece of Allie's discipleship. The rest of it came because every one of us— before, during, and after—reaffirmed the same invitation to that young woman: "Follow Jesus." And that's what she has done.

I began *Disruptive Discipleship* with a basic premise: we can't afford to stay at our current maturity level. An unmoving faith, like a pond with no input or output, grows stagnant. We must be willing to do what we've been too afraid to do or too tired to do, which creates space for God to refresh us. And God will. I've seen it. You've seen it. The Lord loves to do what he is willing and capable of doing.

Fortunately, he's also the one who initiates the process. He says, "It's time to get off the couch, Sam." My job is to say, "Okay." That four-letter word takes effort. Sometimes finances are tight, or the issue is complex. Admitting, "I'm not sure what I need, but I know I need something," requires great courage. The challenges can feel insurmountable. But we must say, "Okay."

Second, I proposed that even a small plan can stir things up. We go for that walk in the cold, or unplug the TV for an evening, or push the lumber cart back into the store. These are the little acts we never graduate from having to do. With practice, we gain confidence to take on larger designs. We have to. Repeating the same small disruptions over and over can become the new routine, either because they lose their novelty or because they no longer match the size of the challenge.

My sister Hope is facing this. She came to visit one weekend, and when I asked about her job, she said, "I feel like I'm heading into a rut."

"Really? Didn't you just graduate?"

"Yes, and I'm already six months into an office job. It's kind of shocking trying to see myself in this thing that won't end until retirement. That's, like, forty-five years from now."

"Well, when you put it that way," I said, laughing. "What are you doing about it?"

"I run errands most evenings, and I'm filling my weekends with activities. I joined a Bible study. I'm going for bike rides, which feels radical to me, but so refreshing. I just slept in a canyon! This isn't normal."

I was happy to hear that she's signing up for new experiences. "Do you like your employer?"

"I do," she said.

"So you're not looking to quit. That's good. What do you think will happen, then, when you've filled every evening and every weekend, when there's no more room for errands or activities?"

For her, this is a big question. Hope knows her current work-play routine will eventually fail to provide the good it provides now; sooner or later it won't match the size of the challenge. I'm encouraged because these small acts will give her confidence to sign up for larger ones when the time comes—like investing in other young employees who find it hard to transition out of college.

Third, we saw that disrupting routine on purpose today builds in us resiliency for unplanned disruptions tomorrow. Whether it's working out or taking reasonable risks, this practice exposes us to new situations and teaches us how to navigate them. In addition, it can unveil aspects of

DISRUPTING ROUTINE ON PURPOSE TODAY BUILDS IN US RESILIENCY FOR UNPLANNED DISRUPTIONS TOMORROW.

how we are made in the image of God, aspects we weren't aware of before. And when the unexpected trial does come, we'll be able to take it on with more joy, as the apostle James implores us to do in James 1:2.

That joy, by the way—to whatever degree we have it—testifies of maturity, for it comes from a place of self-denial and hope. When we are given the strength to refuse a quick fix (self-denial) and when we are given a reason to press on through that refusal (hope), we experience maturity. And that brings joy.

Finally, this discipleship work is done with others. We give; we receive. They give; they receive. The path is with others and toward others, from disciple to disciple maker. Richard Gula wrote, "Since community is necessary to grow in God's image, the fundamental responsibility of being the image of God and for living in community is to give oneself away as completely as possible in imitation of God's self-giving."[15] The body of Christ moves best when it moves together.

My walk with Jesus has looked kind of like a hike, with delightful miles of abundance, ho-hum stretches of valley, and occasional wrong turns. As you read these words, I may even be stuck somewhere. Such are the real ups and downs of being a disciple. But it's a hike, which means the journey keeps going, and that fact reveals a breathtaking truth that I see at every overlook. There, looking back over the miles, I see God's faithfulness sustaining me, calling me out of stuck places, inviting, prodding, revealing, equipping— all the while proving that I'm not where I was last week or the decade before. I am further along. I am stronger. I have more experience to help me deal

THE BODY OF CHRIST MOVES BEST WHEN IT MOVES TOGETHER.

with things that at one time would have crushed me. Specifically because of his faithfulness, I'm growing up. I am truly becoming more like Jesus, and he invites you to do the same. Will you sign up?

Now to him who is able to do immeasurably more than all we ask or imagine, according to his power that is at work within us. (Ephesians 3:20)

EPILOGUE

A Caution for Disciple Makers

In 1998, I left the public school system for broader "classrooms" in the outdoors and on college campuses. I entered nontraditional settings with XD mentors who taught me about emerging design and suspending normal. They showed me how to create space for growth and how to listen for the heart's longings. I took classes, read books, and heard my colleagues ask probing questions to reveal a group's dysfunction and then facilitate the hard work of repairing it. As we applied these skills in restaurants with young professionals and in boardrooms with administrators, it affirmed my interest in seeing Jesus as a facilitator of educational experiences.

In particular, I was awakened to Jesus' brilliant use of surprise to address people's needs—telling fishermen to go against better judgment, switching roles by washing his students' feet, inviting himself over to a tax collector's house (a serious cultural faux pas). This wasn't classroom teaching; this was the Messiah messing with people's routines. And it changed their lives for good. Seeing his unorthodox ways caused me to consider the *how* behind his command to "Go and make disciples of all nations."

Eventually, I learned to create disruptions for others so they could taste the faith, hope, and love I knew was available. Whether leading in a team or alone, I paid close attention and faced whatever

ambiguity attentiveness couldn't resolve. I confronted real and perceived limitations—my own and others'—and tried to prepare
myself for pushback, fear, and even praise. When I got it right,
amazing things happened. These were the transformational moments I had dreamed about.

But there was a caution. The training and experience tempted
me to believe I was in charge of that transformation.

In chapter five, I shared this phrase from theologian David Willis:
"the unfolding realization of God's steadfast love." The kingdom
comes to light—it unfolds—as we collaborate with one another and
with God to do his work. Whatever training we receive or design
we implement, effectiveness is predicated on our attentiveness to
what God is already doing.

I first thought about this approach to effectiveness during a
lecture with campus ministry colleagues, when author M. Craig
Barnes said, "Christ is the one who acts. It's Jesus' job to change the
world, and ours just to witness." As people who considered themselves "change agents," we wondered what he meant. We spent a
good chunk of time encouraging young adults to make a difference
in the world. Many of them were leaders, and leaders initiate change.

Someone asked, "You're saying our job is just to help students
witness, or watch, what Jesus is doing. Isn't that rather passive?"

Barnes gave a simple reply: "Imagine that your student, Joe, becomes an accountant. He's in a meeting when a coworker offers an
unethical financial solution. Joe thinks, *Wait, that's not a good idea.*
That is Jesus coming to the table and saying to him, 'Joe, here is your
chance to jump in and respond to what you see.'" All I could picture
were the classic examples of Christians initiating change: St. Augustine, William Wilberforce, Mother Teresa. They were active
doers, not passive watchers. Right?

Several years later, Barnes's words returned to me when I
stumbled upon a book by C. H. Dodd. Dodd wrote that Old

Testament prophets were change agents in the sense that "their minds were opened to God as well as open to the impact of outward facts"—that is, they watched first. Listen to how Dodd describes a famous scene from the Bible, when Isaiah encountered God's holiness in the temple:

> Imagine, then, the young courtier, deeply concerned with the social and political problems of his country, which is faced by a "demise of the crown" at a time of crisis in international affairs; concerned with these problems, but at a level deeper than that of ordinary political discussion. He has been attending at worship in the Temple, and remains there in meditation, his eyes upon the still smoking altar, and the bizarre carved figures of supernatural beings which we know to have adorned the building.[1]

This was not an account of being blindsided. Isaiah's encounter was certainly terrifying and profoundly humbling. God's holiness revealed the stark contrast between himself and Isaiah, and it elicited the confession "I am ruined!" (Isaiah 6:5). But Dodd seems to convey that Isaiah's encounter was less like the apostle Paul's, who had physically been blinded in an instant by God on the road to Damascus.

Rather, it was more like Nehemiah's, who had been watching diligently for what to do. Let me explain. Nehemiah was in tune with the heart of God and with the state of Israel. He had been watching and had witnessed what was happening to his people. For four months, he prayed to know how to respond (Nehemiah 1:1–2:1). In the same way that Isaiah was, as Dodd said, "deeply concerned with the social and political problems of his country," Nehemiah's mind was "opened to God as well as open to the impact of outward facts." In both cases, these men were humbled and confessed their sins. In both cases, they witnessed God's heart for his people and heard what Joe, the accountant, had heard: "Here is your chance to jump in and respond to what you see."

This is why paying attention had to become more important to me than taking charge. By witnessing what God is up to, we become co-unfolders. We attune ourselves to God, observe the situation at hand, and respond. The result may be that we change the world like Nehemiah, who went to the king with a plan to rebuild Jerusalem's wall, or like Wilberforce, whose dedication led to the abolition of slavery in England, or like Mother Teresa, who inspired millions to care for the needy. None of them initiated these events on their own, per se; they responded to what they saw. Being good students made them good teachers.

Is it true that some of us get to witness God's heart more intimately than others? Isaiah's vision seems wild and supernatural; Nehemiah's was logical and calculated. One is about winged seraphs and smoke; the other is about architectural blueprints and stone. Details aside, maybe they aren't all that different. Dodd's explanation doesn't reduce the power of what occurred to Isaiah, but instead makes it more accessible to us than seems possible. If these guys lived down the street from us today, we might see them as two ordinary believers responding to the times.

In fact, they might be like Amanda, who attended a Jubilee workshop hosted by International Justice Mission (jubileeconference.com). "That was it," she said. "Right there, on the second floor of that conference building, God ignited something in my heart. Fighting human trafficking became my life."[2] The CCO's president, Vince Burens, relayed the story in a staff newsletter:

> Amanda returned to campus, started an IJM campus chapter, and learned as much as she could about the issue. . . . She learned that the largest gap in services for survivors was legal representation. So she went to law school, and then set up an

internship in Thailand to end child prostitution. She now works in Dallas with immigrants, including screening for children who may be victims of violence or human trafficking.

Was Amanda blindsided like Paul, or had she been watching like Nehemiah? Or was it some combination of the two, like Isaiah? Regardless, these stories ought to encourage us, for they remind us that growth for the attentive and humble follower of Christ lies right around the bend. We are not in charge of that growth. We are not able to transform others. But the transformational insight that's revealed commissions us to invite others to be transformed.

ACKNOWLEDGMENTS

Al Hsu, you are a fine editor. More importantly, you pulled my thoughts together at a scary diner in Pittsburgh and gave me a chance to write this book. You couldn't have known it, but that little meeting contributed to the close of my midlife transition.

Marcus Goodyear, you and I sat together the night before. It was late, and I asked why I should keep my meeting with Al in the morning. "I've been slogging through a heavy season," I said. "I'm not ready to start a book—I don't even have an idea for a book. What am I supposed to tell him?" You encouraged me to go anyway, and you said you'd pray. Thank you for being a good friend and for sharpening my writing over the years, this book included.

Erica Young Reitz, you emailed me with news that InterVarsity Press was interested in *After College*, and then you asked if I wanted to meet Al when he came to town. You said it would be good for me and that I had something to say. Thank you for insisting.

John Nesbitt, as my spiritual director, how many hours did we sit in your office as you walked me through that tough season? Thank you for asking countless good questions, for listening deeply, processing thoroughly, and praying diligently. I wouldn't have said yes to Erica if it weren't for your guidance.

Paul Harbison, a group of us gathered weekly in the late nineties to hear what you had to say about experiential education. I was young. I wanted to transform college students. You said I needed to be transformed first. Thank you for practicing what you preach. You have always believed that thoughtful, challenging, well-designed experiences create space for God to transform us. Because of that belief, I continue to sign up for them.

To all of my colleagues in the CCO, especially François Guilleux and the CCO's XD department, thank you for sharpening me. How true it is that faithfulness is pursued together!

To Lisa and George Foose, and to places like Pine Springs Camp, I am thankful for the early investment that allowed me to take risks and to learn from my mistakes.

To the hardworking crew at InterVarsity Press, you live out your faith through excellent work. Thank you for taking on this project.

To friends on social media and down the street, thank you for sharing stories about your own discipleship and for encouraging me through this process.

To my CCO donors, who have supported this work that makes disciples, thank you. No, seriously, this book and its stories and the people I'm thanking and my career for the past twenty years never would have happened without you. You are manna from heaven.

And to Julie, Emma, and Alice, the experience of being a family with you has been simultaneously wonderful and grounding. Where else can I have so much fun and yet see so clearly where I still need to grow? I love you.

DISRUPTIVE DISCIPLESHIP WITH OTHERS

It can be tough to get unstuck, especially by yourself. When my friend Scott invited us to the diner to confess that he was in a slump, he wanted to move forward *together*. Below is a conversation guide for you and a few friends to use with this book. Consider it a disruptive design—a self-appointed intervention of sorts where you invite people in and give them permission to ask questions. If you have a friend in need, offer this to him or her.

Either way, as it has been said before, the body of Christ moves best when it moves together.

Here are a few suggestions:

- Keep the group size between two and nine.
- Establish a consistent time and place to meet.
- Listen well. Listening almost always beats talking.[1] Even when it's time for advice, few people enjoy being pounced on.
- Pray for each other between meetings.

INTRODUCTION: WE CAN'T NOT CHANGE

Read: James 1:3-4

1. What's wrong with the classic yearbook advice "Don't ever change"?

2. Which reader are you most like: (a) stuck and wants to be unstuck, (b) serving Jesus but wanting more, or (c) about to enter a transition? Maybe something different?

3. What's wrong with staying where you are?

4. When have you experienced a kick-start before. What came of it?

5. What will you need in order to read this book? (Time? Help? Discipline? Something else?)

6. Who needs to read this book with you?

Pray: "Jesus, it's easy to be comfortable, but I want to be mature and complete. Will you help me?"

Act: If you haven't already done it, invite a few others to meet with you. Their collaboration will lend insight and encouragement.

CHAPTER 1: FEELING STUCK

Read: Mark 10:46-52

1. Sam's grandfather had a ratty lawn chair that needed to be fixed or tossed, but he was too stuck to do either. Can you think of something like that chair in your own life?

2. What is the connection between being stuck and being immature?

3. How does being stuck affect others?

4. Name one or two people who have been (or currently are) affected by you being stuck?

5. How long has it been since you asked someone for help?

6. Though blind, Bartimaeus recognized Jesus and called out to him. Jesus responded, "What do you want me to do for you?" How would you reply?

Pray: "Lord, by your mercy, I believe you are inviting me to something. Thank you. I want to say yes. It's time to say yes."

Act: Write an invitation to yourself from God.

CHAPTER 2: EXPLORING OPTIONS

Read: Exodus 4:10-13

1. On a scale of one to ten, ten being *very*, how open are you to new experiences? Tell a story about a time when a new experience ended poorly.

2. Everyone has a threshold for discomfort. What happens when you cross yours?

3. What happens when you don't?

4. Of the three design types—diagnostic, prescriptive, and preparatory—which type seems to address the area you need to grow in? (Think about how you answered Jesus' question to Bartimaeus under chapter one. Consider that as the area you need to grow in.)

5. What is one fear that threatens to keep you where you are?

6. Name one hope that makes you want to move from a B-minus (or a D-minus) life to a B-plus life.

Pray: "God, you promise new land for me—not in a wealth-and-power kind of way, but in a way that represents an expansion of maturity and freedom from captivity. Free me from whatever keeps me where I am."

Act: This week, address your fear. Own it, confess it, and surrender it.

CHAPTER 3: MAKING A PLAN

Read: Luke 14:28-30; 15:17-20

1. Some people are disinclined to plan. If this is you, what would help?

2. Why is it important to ask questions?

3. Discuss "Jesus loves doers." Does he love them more than couch potatoes? Does he love you when you are the couch potato? If there is a discrepancy between your answers, why?

4. Of the five details—purpose, shape, time, cost, and location— which is most important to you? Are there other points you need to add to this list?

5. What temptations could affect your design (for example, the desire for bragging rights)?

6. What will it take to sign up?

Pray: "Father, I don't need to prove anything to you. You love me just as I am. Please bless this plan I'm working on, and if you have something else in mind, grant me the serenity to let this plan go. May these efforts honor you."

Act: Begin filling out a "Design Criteria for a Disruptive Experience" from appendix B.

CHAPTER 4: STEPPING OUT IN FAITH

Read: Exodus 16:22-30

1. Imagine you were part of the group Sam left in the dark. What was the experience like for you? What role did you play? Did your relationship with him change during the activity? (See Sara's and Eve's responses at the end of the chapter for reference.)

2. Name two comfort areas in your life where you do not have to exercise faith in God.

3. Are faith and risk related? What does your relationship with risk say about your faith?

4. What people or past experiences have shaped your faith the most?

5. Based on your understanding of God, how able are you to move "from false certainties to true uncertainties"?

6. What do you need for the middle ground, and what has Jesus already given you to do it?

Pray: "Thank you, Savior, for my limitations. They remind me that I need you. Even when I act bravely or heroically, I know that I can't save myself. Will you increase my faith?"

Act: Pick an item from "Do It: Designs to Grow in Faith" at the end of chapter four.

CHAPTER 5: REDISCOVERING HOPE

Read: Romans 8:25

1. What kind of trouble can self-reliance cause?

2. Paul suggests that hope requires patience. Does patience come easily to you or not?

3. How do promises fulfilled and promises broken affect your ability to hope?

4. Shawn Smucker confessed that when challenges come, his temptation "is to make drastic changes." How does hope affect your own response?

5. What makes you quit? And what is the cost of quitting?

6. When Simeon held the Christ child in the temple, what do you think that did for him? What do you hope the risen Christ will do for you?

Pray: "God, you said, 'I will do it.' Sometimes that is hard to believe. There is so much brokenness in the world—and in my own life, too. But today is a new day. Will you encourage me to hold on, like the flag-form spruce?"

Act: Pick an item from "Do It: Designs to Grow in Hope" at the end of chapter five.

CHAPTER 6: GROWING IN LOVE

Read: Luke 10:38-42

1. When it comes to love, are you more like Sam when Miriam had an asthma attack or Juancito when he washed dishes in the stream?

2. Some people get your best; others get your worst. You might be gracious to one and nagging to another, hospitable to one and hurtful to another. Why?

3. What could happen to those who get your worst if you don't mature?

4. Martha chose to make preparations for Jesus instead of sitting at his feet like her sister, Mary. How do you show love, and what might Jesus say about it?

5. How would things change if your career were driven by love first?

6. Even after seeing our need, it can still feel impossible to grow. What small way has Jesus encouraged you toward love in the past? How might that indication lend courage to you in the future?

Pray: "Lamb of God, you died for me and for the people in my life. I don't understand this gift, but I am grateful. Teach me how to pay it forward so that your gift may increase."

Act: Pick an item from "Do It: Designs to Grow in Love" at the end of chapter six.

CHAPTER 7: TRANSLATING CHANGE

Read: Luke 10:25-37

1. How might traveling far away equip you to live better next door?

2. Are you best at translation, transference, or integration?

3. Describe two situations where these three came together well for you. For the first, give a basic example, like how you learned not to touch the stove when it's hot. For the second, give a more complex example, like how you learned to respond to a problematic boss.

4. When have translation, transference, and integration *not* come together, and you ended up like the contestant on *Wipeout* who got slammed by the door three times?

5. Why is transference so important and so difficult at the same time?

6. If Jesus said to you, "Go and do likewise," what specifically would he be telling you to do?

Pray: "Jesus, as a teacher, you were constantly trying to help people see more clearly. Will you give me eyes to see and ears to hear, so I can live out what I learn?"

Act: Read the story of the good Samaritan again. Ask, "How might Jesus retell this story, with me in my current life as the good Samaritan?" Think about how you would "go and do likewise" at work, in your family, in your neighborhood, and possibly even in yourself. Then go and do it.

CHAPTER 8: NAVIGATING VALLEYS

Read: 1 Kings 19:1-15

1. Do you grow more from planned disruptions or unplanned ones? Which would you rather experience?

2. Midlife and quarter-life can be tough stretches to endure.[2] But losing a job, your health, or a family member can happen at any time. How do you deal with challenges?

3. What's going on right now that feels like the valley to you, and what do you need?

4. Jesus said, "Deny yourself" (Matthew 16:24). Is it fair for him to require this?

5. What did Jesus hold onto when he suffered? What gave him hope?

6. Referring to the idol illustrations in this chapter, what mimics the truth for you, and what would it take to turn away from it?

Pray: "Holy Spirit, you are wisdom. Lead me through this maze. I don't know the way out."

Act: Go for a walk in the cemetery. As you enter, lay down whatever weight you shouldn't be carrying. When you leave, ask for new life.

CHAPTER 9: GETTING UNSTUCK TOGETHER

Read: 1 Corinthians 12:12-26

1. Who do you turn to for help?
2. Who have you helped?
3. None of us is perfect at receiving and giving. Which side do you favor?
4. How does your preference for receiving or giving affect your relationships?
5. What part do you play in the body of Christ, and how adequate do you feel in that role?
6. In what ways is community as difficult as it is beautiful?

Pray: "My King, you have made me one of your people. Now please make me a good citizen who loves with all my heart, mind, soul, and strength."

Act: Let someone help you this week. Then thank that person. Or go out of your way for somebody this week—enough that it costs you. (Pick the more difficult option.)

Appendix A

WHAT JESUS KNEW ABOUT EXPERIENTIAL EDUCATION

A Bible Study

There are various ways to interpret the Road to Emmaus story in Luke 24:13-35. This one offers a two-part reminder that aligns with the message of *Disruptive Discipleship*: (1) Jesus cares about getting us unstuck, and (2) we can follow his lead in helping others do the same. Whether it's through direct honesty, playful creativity, or in this case, gradual epiphany, making disciples is something we can do, too.

SUMMARY

We grow in our bike-riding skills by riding a bike. We learn our way around the kitchen by cooking. In a similar way, we mature in our faith through experience. Jesus knew this. He loved to teach through experience, and he used this method frequently. In this lesson, we'll look at how he did it and what we can learn by watching him at work.

BIBLE DISCUSSION

Leader. The following Bible discussion involves two distraught disciples and one clever, caring Teacher. You're going to help the group focus on how Jesus' teaching methods opened the eyes of the disciples. It's okay if you are still learning about this topic. Just be humble and learn along with the group. The lesson here—from the story and for you—is this: how you communicate a message is almost as important as the message itself.

Read. Jesus frequently used out-of-the-ordinary teaching methods to get a lesson across. Just think about the time he drew on the ground as he addressed Pharisees who had caught a woman in adultery (John 8:1-11). Or think about how he healed the crippled woman on the Sabbath day instead of the day after or the day before. She'd been crippled for eighteen years—couldn't he have picked a different day? Not if he wanted to heal her *and* the religious elite. Let's turn to another story where Jesus demonstrates his knowledge of experiential education.

Ask.

+ Will someone in the group please read Luke 24:13-35 for us?
+ What teaching methods did Jesus use in this story? See if you can come up with at least five. [He asked questions, walked beside them (didn't stand in front of them), talked with them (didn't talk over them), challenged their reasoning, lectured from the Scriptures, put on a charade, etc.]
+ How did his style engage the two disciples? [His hospitality made them comfortable, his knowledge made them interested, etc.]
+ What role did the Holy Spirit play in his interaction with them? [The Holy Spirit complements Jesus' words and actions by convicting the disciples.]

ARTICLE

Leader. Ask your group to read the following out loud, taking turns every paragraph or so.

By all accounts, Jesus was brilliant. That much is clear. It's *how* he carried out that brilliance that often makes me shake my head. No matter what challenge came his way, he proved not only to be on top of things but also to be clever in the process. There are two particular ways I see this. First, he could turn any challenge into a teachable moment, which made him an unrivaled educator. Second, he loved to teach through experience.

Here is an example. Jesus could have said to his disciples, "You need my help." Instead, he waited until late one afternoon when a large crowd grew hungry and the disciples asked him to send the people away to buy food. He replied, "You give them something to eat" (Mark 6:37). Do you see what he did? It's brilliant. He forced the disciples into an impossible situation in which they needed his help. He didn't have to tell them with words. They felt it, and then they saw it when he fed the crowd himself. Their experience proved that they needed him.

Let's look at another example, this one involving Jesus' brilliance in how he cares for us in hard times. This example requires an introduction.

There are moments in life when faith falls out of its old container. Heading off to college can cause this. Being unemployed can cause this. Losing a loved one can cause this. What once worked—comfortably, I might add—suddenly doesn't. The neat little box that held all of faith's parts in one organized place cracks across the bottom, and the pieces spill onto the floor. It might seem fine to simply grab another box and stuff it all back in, but now that it's sprawled out in plain sight, you're able to make several observations: (1) there seems to be less there than you assumed, (2) pieces are missing, and (3) you don't know how to proceed.

Ronald Rolheiser wrote, "In the discouragement that ensues we will be tempted to walk away from our faith . . . toward some place of consolation."[1] Here's the thing. You need something to hold life together when life falls apart. Even if what you're going through isn't a crisis, the lack of control and inability to predict the future can have a similar effect. These tough moments send you looking (quickly, desperately, foolishly) for anything to resemble what you once had. That "anything" is what Rolheiser calls "consolation."

You need something to hold life together when life falls apart.

This is precisely what happened after Jesus' crucifixion. The long-awaited Messiah had finally come, and with promise, healing, and hope, too. He filled faith boxes to the brim and more, and then, just like that, he was gone, and the pieces were beginning to fall out. Disciples hid, doubts set in, opposition rejoiced. Nobody really knew what to do.

The scene picks up in Luke 24:13, on a seven-mile walk from Jerusalem to the village of Emmaus. Two disciples, with "faces downcast," talked "with each other about everything that had happened." The resurrected Jesus joined them, but they didn't recognize him. This is key, so keep it in mind. When asked for more information, they demonstrated a mix of sadness and confusion. On one hand, they were amazed by the women disciples, who said they had seen a vision of angels, who said he was alive. On the other, they confessed, "We had hoped that he was the one who was going to redeem Israel" (v. 21). There were pieces all over the ground.

Rolheiser called Emmaus their consolation. It is their home, their familiar, their place of relative semblance of order. Maybe life is predictable in Emmaus for these two. They have a place to stay and food to eat. They *know* it. And it is en route to this place that Jesus joins them—full of grace and generous in his practice of leaving the ninety-nine to find the one (Matthew 18:12).

It's interesting to watch how Jesus joined them, because he didn't do it all at once. Why not? Well, remember that they didn't recognize him. We might even say they *could not* recognize him. Rolheiser wrote, "Their faith had trained their eyes to see and recognize only a Christ who fit their understanding and imagination" (the old container). "A crucified Jesus did not fit into that understanding and thus was unrecognizable to them, even as he was chatting with them."[2] Israel's hope and their Savior had just died. Recognizing him—here and now and raised from the dead!—exceeded their capacity. So what was Jesus to do? He would have to take it slowly.

Luke 24:28 reads, "As they approached the village to which they were going, Jesus continued on as if he were going farther." What a fascinating phrase! Maybe it was good etiquette that he didn't invite himself over. I believe this bit of acting was for a different reason. Following a compelling and lengthy conversation along the road, acting "as if he were going farther" created a moment of separation. Perhaps you know the feeling from an evening with friends, when one person decides to leave, and you recognize immediately whether it feels too early, delayed, or just right. This feeling also tells you whether (and how much) you were having a good time, a boring time, or a just-right time. "But they urged him strongly" (v. 29) indicates they'd been having a *very good time*. The separation announcement had its desired effect. They were beginning to recognize something—not Jesus yet, but something.

Jesus played on this growing curiosity and proceeded to disclose himself even more during the breaking of bread, until "their eyes were opened" (v. 31). Not until after he had gone did they finally put it all together. They could see the new container he had left there on the table.

"They got up and returned at once to Jerusalem" (v. 33).

DISCUSSION

Leader. Your job here is to help the group members make connections between the Bible story, the article, and their own lives. Use the questions below to get started.

Ask.

• Think about a time when your eyes were opened. Did it happen in the classroom or through an experience? (Invite a few to share their story.) [Ask clarifying questions, such as "Was there a teacher or facilitator involved?" "How did that person's style contribute to the experience?"]

• Do you agree or disagree with Sam about why Jesus acted "as if he were going farther" (Luke 24:28)? Are there other reasons Luke may have been inspired to include this phrase?

• Jesus called us to be disciples as well as to make disciples. What is your preferred method for teaching, instructing, or influencing others? How does Jesus' method(s) encourage your growth in this area?

EXERCISE

Leader. Divide your group into smaller groups. To each, assign one of the following teaching methods. Try to use at least three:

• Classroom lecture

• Postmodern conversation ("Truth is relative, so believe what you want, and I'll believe what I want.")

• Skit

• Socratic method (a series of questions that help people discover their beliefs about a topic)

• Personal storytelling

Give the groups three minutes to prepare a retelling of Luke 24:13-35 according to their assigned teaching method. The point isn't to rewrite every line, but to provide a taste of how the story might have gone if Jesus had chosen a different method.

Give each group two minutes to present their retelling.

Ask.

• Which group offered the most compelling retelling?

• Why did Jesus choose the method he did?

WRAP UP

Ask. Do you have any questions or comments?

Pray. Invite someone to close the meeting with an open prayer or to read the prayer below. If no one volunteers after five seconds, offer to do it.

Jesus, thank you for showing yourself to the disciples along the road. Their faith was falling apart, and you walked with them in their pain and then healed their pain. Sometimes we need to walk a lot further before you show up. In those times and even in the good times, help us to be ready for whatever experience or experiences you need to use in order to restore us. You are a brilliant and caring teacher, and we ask that we would be willing and patient students. Finally, we pray, inspire us to pay attention to how we teach others, showing the same care and creativity that you did. Amen.

Appendix B

DESIGN TEMPLATES FOR DISCIPLE MAKERS

In this appendix, you'll find three slightly different templates for creating a design: one for personal use, one for leading a group, and one for helping another person. You may have different ways of doing this—including better or more thorough ways. These are only templates. They have proven to be useful, but please adapt them to your own style and situation.

For the second two—leading a group and helping another person—you'll be playing the role of guide or facilitator. See the list of resources afterward, where you'll find readings, websites, tools, and programs that may help in your ongoing growth as a disciple maker.

TEMPLATE I: DESIGNING FOR PERSONAL GROWTH

Use the following template for yourself. Fill it out with a person who cares about you. Take a few days to answer the first two questions. Ask your guide to offer feedback in case you are skirting an issue or not seeing clearly. Then take a week to complete the details. (A small design could be completed in a few hours—the idea is to promote thoughtfulness.) Once you finish, ask your guide to help in other ways if necessary, perhaps with a recommendation or to pull strings or to lend camping supplies or the key to a cabin.

What's the issue I'm facing? Is it complacency? Anxiety? Not enough financial self-discipline? Greed? Insecurity? Fear? Where am I stuck, and how is it affecting my faith (the belief that God *can*), my hope (the belief that God *will*), or my love (the behavior toward God and others that demonstrates my beliefs)? Where can I get additional insight about me?

Recommendations. Pray. Explore each role you play, such as sister, father, employee. Ask an honest friend what he or she sees going on in you.

What type of design could get me unstuck and promote growth in this area?

- Pick *diagnostic* if you aren't sure what the issue is.
- Pick *prescriptive* if you know where you're stuck and you need help getting out.
- Pick *preparatory* to train for a known or unknown challenge in the future.

What details will make this design a reality?

Purpose.

KEY QUESTION: Why this design for this issue?

Shape.

KEY QUESTION: What should my disruption look like?

PROMPTS: Retreat? Fast? Road trip? Alone or with others?

Time.

KEY QUESTION: How much time will it require?

PROMPTS: Length? Start date? Frequency? Travel to get there? Time needed from others?

Cost.

KEY QUESTION: How should this disruption cost me

- financially?
- physically?
- mentally?
- socially?
- spiritually?

PROMPT: How much "normal" should I suspend?

Location.

KEY QUESTION: Where should this experience take place?

PROMPTS: Far? Near? In a desert to highlight thirst? In a city to face people fears?

Use the "Design Criteria for a Disruptive Experience" questions at the end of this appendix to see how your plan measures up. Make adjustments until it does before signing up.

Sign up!

TEMPLATE 2: DESIGNING FOR A GROUP

Use the following template to design a group experience. Whenever possible, collaborate with one or more partners who can balance your perspective.

What is the issue being faced? Is it communication? Work ethic? Conflict avoidance? Fear? Trust? Pending changes in the group's leadership or organizational structure? What signs or symptoms indicate the need for growth? How could faith, hope, and love help?

What type of design could get them unstuck and promote growth in this area?

- Pick *diagnostic* if you aren't sure what the issue is.

- Pick *prescriptive* if you know where they're stuck, and they need help getting out.
- Pick *preparatory* to train for a known or unknown challenge in the future.

What details will make this design a reality?

Purpose.

KEY QUESTION: Why this design for this issue?

Shape.

KEY QUESTION: What should the disruption look like?

PROMPTS: A staff retreat? Role-playing scenarios? Team-building activities?

Time.

KEY QUESTION: How much time will it require?

PROMPTS: Length? Start date? Frequency? Travel to get there?

Cost.

KEY QUESTION: How should this disruption cost them

- financially?
- physically?
- mentally?
- socially?
- spiritually?

PROMPT: How much "normal" should be suspended?

Location.

KEY QUESTION: Where should this experience take place?

PROMPTS: Far? Near? In an escape room to address collaboration?

Use the "Design Criteria for a Disruptive Discipleship" questions to see how the plan measures up. Make adjustments if necessary.

Sign up!

TEMPLATE 3: GUIDING AN INDIVIDUAL

Use the following template as a discipleship tool with someone. You may choose to work through the questions together in one meeting, or spread it out. A simple design can be completed in a couple of hours. If it's more complex, give the person a week to reflect on the first two questions. Offer feedback if he or she skirts an issue or can't see clearly. Then give another week or two to complete the details. Once you give the green light, assist if necessary. He or she may need a recommendation or for you to pull strings. If it's appropriate, share some of the cost: entrance fee, cabin rental, the keys to your motorcycle.

What is the issue you're facing? Is it complacency? Anxiety? Not enough financial self-discipline? Greed? Insecurity? Fear? Where are you stuck, and how is it affecting your faith (your belief that God *can*), your hope (your belief that God *will*), or your love (your behavior toward God and others that demonstrates your beliefs)? Jesus asked Bartimaeus, "What do you want me to do for you?" (Mark 10:36). How would *you* answer him?

Recommendations. Pray. Explore each role you play, such as sister, father, employee. Ask an honest friend what he or she sees going on in you.

What type of design could get you unstuck and promote growth in this area?

- Pick *diagnostic* if you aren't sure what you need help with.
- Pick *prescriptive* if you know where you're stuck and you need help getting out.
- Pick *preparatory* to train for a known or unknown challenge in the future.

What details will make this design a reality?

Purpose.

KEY QUESTION: Why this design for this issue?

Shape.

KEY QUESTION: What should your disruption look like?

PROMPTS: Retreat? Fast? Trip? Alone or with others?

Time.

KEY QUESTION: How much time will it require?

PROMPTS: Length? Start date? Frequency? Travel to get there? Time needed from others?

Cost.

KEY QUESTION: How should this disruption cost you

- financially?
- physically?
- mentally?
- socially?
- spiritually?

PROMPT: How much "normal" should you suspend?

Location.

KEY QUESTION: Where should this experience take place?

PROMPTS: Far? Near? In a cabin for solitude? On a rock wall for courage?

Check the "Design Criteria for a Disruptive Discipleship" questions to see how the plan measures up. Help with adjustments until it does.

Sign up!

DESIGN CRITERIA FOR A DISRUPTIVE EXPERIENCE

Yeses are what you are looking for. If there aren't enough, keep tweaking the details.

Yes	No	*Key Question*
		Does it exist with a purpose? Do you know what that purpose is?
		Will it allow for challenge-by-choice, when applicable? (Everyone has limits, and while we should be encouraged to overcome fears, we should also be able to opt out within reason.)
		Will it disrupt routine and comfort?
		Will it include risk or at least the perception of risk?
		Will it promote collaboration if others are involved?
		Will it test current understandings and/or skills?
		Will it demand flexibility and persistence?
		Will it require application of new understanding and/or skills?
		Will it provide space for reflection?
		Will its conclusions be transferable to daily life?

ADDITIONAL RESOURCES FOR DISCIPLE MAKERS

This list of readings, websites, tools, and trainings contains items that have been helpful to others and me in our work as disciple makers. The list is obviously incomplete (and biased), so be sure to consider your experience, as well as your ministry context. Every disciple maker and disciple should be reading and studying the Bible on a regular basis.

Reading

Bolsinger, Tod. *Canoeing the Mountains: Christian Leadership in Uncharted Territory.* Downers Grove, IL: InterVarsity Press, 2015.

Breen, Mike. *Building a Discipling Culture.* 2nd ed. Pawley's Island, SC: 3DM Publishing, 2011.

Heifetz, Ronald A. *Leadership Without Easy Answers.* Cambridge, MA: Harvard University Press, 1994.

Kalisch, Kenneth R. *The Role of the Instructor in the Outward Bound Educational Process.* Kearney, NE: Morris Publishing, 1999.

Miller, Sherod, and Phyllis A. Miller. *Core Communication: Skills and Process.* Evergreen, CO: Interpersonal Communication Programs, 1997.

Mullarkey, Christine, and Kelly S. Bloom. *Project GO: Facilitation Manual.* Sacramento, CA: Project Great Outdoors, 2009. www .projectgo.org/cms/wp-content/uploads/2012/08/FacilitationLR1 .pdf.

Nouwen, Henri J. M. *Reaching Out: The Three Movements of the Spiritual Life.* New York: Image, 1975.

Palmer, Parker J. "Leading from Within: Reflections on Spirituality and Leadership." Washington, DC: The Servant Leadership School, 1990.

Scandrette, Mark. *Practicing the Way of Jesus: Life Together in the Kingdom of Love.* Downers Grove, IL: InterVarsity Press, 2011.

Scazzero, Peter. *Emotionally Healthy Spirituality: Unleashing the Power of Authentic Life in Christ.* Nashville: Thomas Nelson, 2006.

Websites

Tools and tips for leading groups: liberatingstructures.com.

Prayer: centeringprayer.com. According to spiritual director Shelly Reimersma, "Thomas Keating's books and practices have helped me to let people learn and grow at a pace that is right for them in their development, and not insist on their growth for my own needs."

Tools and trainings

Core Communications. This two-day intrapersonal communication program teaches six talking skills and five listening skills that aid in the resolution of conflict, in decision making, and in effective negotiation. Based on Dr. Sharod Miller and Dr. Phyllis Miller's book *Core Communication: Skills and Process.* Visit ccojubilee.org/xd-professional-development/.

Working with Groups. Frequently offered in conjunction with Core Communications, this interactive seminar integrates theory and practice to teach how to read, understand, evaluate, and effectively lead groups. Three to four days. Visit ccojubilee.org/xd-professional-development/.

Situational Leadership Model. This model "provides leaders with an understanding of the relationship between an effective style of leadership and the level of readiness followers exhibit for a specific task." Useful for knowing how to disciple (and when) according to individual learning styles versus approaching everyone in the same way. Visit situational.com/the-cls-difference/situational-leadership-what-we-do/.

Intercultural Development Inventory. The IDI "assesses intercultural competence—the capability to shift cultural perspective and appropriately adapt behavior to cultural differences and commonalities." This tool is useful if you serve or work in crosscultural contexts, whether locally or internationally. See idiinventory.com.

Leadership Circle Profile. This tool "helps leaders understand the relationship between how they habitually think, how they behave, and, more importantly, how all this impacts their current level of leadership effectiveness." Go to leadershipcircle.com/assessment-tools /profile/.

NOTES

INTRODUCTION

[1]Read the story at www.pitt.edu/~dash/grimm145.html.

[2]Read Dietrich Bonhoeffer's *The Cost of Discipleship* to learn more about that cost.

[3]If you're a recent grad, read Erica Young Reitz's practical and relevant *After College: Navigating Transitions, Relationships and Faith* (Downers Grove, IL: InterVarsity Press, 2016).

1 FEELING STUCK

[1]J. R. R. Tolkien's portrayal of Gollum and the One Ring in *The Lord of the Rings* comes to mind here. Gollum became so attached to his "Precious" that it destroyed him.

[2]Dr. Michael Hurd, "What the Heck Is a Corrective Emotional Experience?," DrHurd.com, August 5, 2012, drhurd.com/2013/08/05/what-the-heck-is-a-corrective-emotional-experience/.

[3]Gregg A. Ten Elshof, *I Told Me So: Self-Deception and the Christian Life* (Grand Rapids: Eerdmans, 2009), 46.

[4]Email conversation with Paul Johns, November 26, 2016.

2 EXPLORING OPTIONS

"A Journeying Prayer" by Andy Freeman and Pete Greig in *Punk Monk* (Ventura, CA: Regal, 2007), 180.

[1]Mark Scandrette, *Practicing the Way of Jesus: Life Together in the Kingdom of Love* (Downers Grove, IL: InterVarsity Press, 2011), 59.

[2]Ibid., 60.

[3]His invitation began as a joke for the sake of comparison. It had been years since he lived in the inner city. Still, the idea intrigued me, and we talked about it until he graduated and moved on. I regret not having been able to work it out.

[4]*Scaredy Squirrel,* "A Squirreled Away Treasure," season 1, episode 24 (November 30, 2011).

[5]The lengthier the experience, the more preparations we make. For weekend activities, an email or two may suffice. For three-week international trips to Peru, India, or New Zealand, we begin months in advance, with live and virtual meetings, itinerary discussions, theme-based readings, ongoing prayer, and individual phone calls. In this way, we are able to set the tone spiritually and mentally, and to create a space of readiness.

[6]In Kyle Idleman, *AHA: The God Moment That Changes Everything* (Colorado Springs, CO: David C. Cook, 2014), 192-96.

[7]This question can be tough for those who are planning-challenged. I know my car needs preventive maintenance, but I'm more likely to wait till it breaks and then fix it. (Could there be a prescriptive design in this?)

[8]*The Princess Bride,* directed by Rob Reiner (1987; Beverly Hills, CA: Act III Communications).

[9]Scandrette, *Practicing the Way,* 77.

[10]You can find ready-made designs on the Internet or through friends, or by perusing XD's forty-page catalog. That might do the trick, and you can sign up today. But can I suggest taking the slower route? Chapter three highlights the importance of digging in before signing up, something every wise leader has convinced me to do.

3 MAKING A PLAN

[1]Kyle Idleman, *AHA: The God Moment That Changes Everything* (Colorado Springs, CO: David C. Cook, 2014).

[2]Visit the Right Question Institute at www.rightquestion.org.

[3]Email conversation with Al Hsu, August 8, 2016.

[4]Phillipa Lally et al., "How Are Habits Formed: Modelling Habit Formation in the Real World," *European Journal of Social Psychology* 40, no.6 (October 2010): 998-1009, doi: 10.1002/ejsp.674.

[5]For solitude and beauty, wouldn't visiting a place like the Quiet House be wonderful? "Located on the H. E. Butt Family Foundation property, the Quiet House provides an opportunity for silence, stillness, meditation, and prayer for an individual or a married couple," laitylodge.org/thequi ethouse.

[6]Email conversation with Al Hsu, August 8, 2016.

[7]Watch Cat tell the story in "Experience Life: Finding your way in India," Vimeo, vimeo.com/109740568.

[8]John Dewey, *Experience & Education* (New York: First Touchstone Edition, 1997), 25.

[9]The original title was "A Christian Tin-Can Theory of Man," June 1981, and it can be found at www.allofliferedeemed.co.uk/Seerveld /Seerveld%20_A_Christian_Tin-Can_Theory_of_Man.pdf.

[10]To inquire about purchasing a set of the cards used, go to ccojubilee.org /about-cco-xd.

[11]Craig G. Bartholomew and Michael W. Goheen, *Christian Philosophy: A Systematic and Narrative Introduction* (Grand Rapids: Baker Academic, 2013), 250.

[12]Jack Mezirow, "Transformative Learning: Theory to Practice," *New Directions for Adult and Continuing Education* 74 (1997): 6, www.esludwig .com/uploads/2/6/1/0/26105457/transformative-learning-mezirow -1997.pdf.

[13]Ibid., 10.

[14]M. K. Smith, "David A. Kolb on Experiential Learning," The Encyclopedia of Informal Education, infed.org/mobi/david-a-kolb-on-experiential -learning/. The ELM is cyclical and may not always follow the sequence I show here. It is also often paired with Kolb's Learning Styles Inventory 4.0. See "Learning styles describe your preferred approach to the Learning Cycle," Institute for Experiential Learning, www.experiential learninginstitute.org/learning-cycles-and-styles/.

[15]There are physiological benefits to this as well. For scientific support, see Kelly McGonigal's TED talk "How to Make Stress Your Friend," at www .ted.com/talks/kelly_mcgonigal_how_to_make_stress_your_friend #t-535581.

4 STEPPING OUT IN FAITH

[1]Henri J. M. Nouwen, *Reaching Out: The Three Movement of the Spiritual Life* (New York: Image, 1975), 126.

[2]Email conversation with Paul Johns, September 12, 2016.

[3]For some, settling down may be the hard decision to make, not the glamorous one. See Jonathan Wilson-Hartgrove, *The Wisdom of Stability: Rooting Faith in a Mobile Culture* (Brewster, MA: Paraclete Press, 2010).

[4]Ronald Heifetz, Alexander Grashow, and Marty Linsky, *The Practice of Adaptive Leadership: Tools and Tactics for Changing Your Organization and the World* (Boston: Harvard Business Press, 2009), 17.

[5]"American Donor Trends," Barna, June 3, 2013, barna.com/research /american-donor-trends/.

[6]See Mike Holmes, "What Would Happen if the Church Tithed?," *Relevant*, March 8, 2016, www.relevantmagazine.com/god/church/what -would-happen-if-church-tithed.

5 REDISCOVERING HOPE

[1]Rachel Zurer, "Falling in Love on the Trail," *Backpacker*, September 2015, www.backpacker.com/trips/falling-in-love-on-the-trail.

[2]Watch complete episodes at www.history.com/shows/alone. Note: stressful situations and some profanity.

[3]*Bicycling*, September 2015, 18.

[4]Shawn Smucker, "Five Things I Do Instead of Blowing Up My Life and Starting Over," March 24, 2016, shawnsmucker.com/2016/03/five -things-i-do-instead-of-blowing-up-my-life-and-starting-over/.

[5]William Bridge, *A Lifting Up for the Downcast* (Louisville, KY: GLH Publishing, 2014), 42.

[6]*Backpacker*, March 2015, 36.

[7]"List of Mount Everest Records," Wikipedia, last modified September 14, 2016, en.wikipedia.org/wiki/List_of_Mount_Everest_records.

[8]David Willis, *Notes on the Holiness of God* (Grand Rapids: Eerdmans, 2002), 76.

[9]Ibid., 68.

[10]As of February 2016, that record is held by Aleix Segura Vendrell at twenty-four minutes and three seconds. "Longest time breath held vol-

untarily (male)," Guinness World Records, www.guinnessworldrecords
.com/world-records/longest-time-breath-held-voluntarily-(male).

6 GROWING IN LOVE

[1]Henri J. M. Nouwen, *Reaching Out: The Three Movement of the Spiritual Life* (New York: Image, 1975), 119.

[2]For helpful crosscultural tips, see Michelle Acker Perez, "Things No One Tells You About Going on Short-Term Mission Trips," *Relevant*, May 9, 2016, www.relevantmagazine.com/reject-apathy/things-no-one-tells -you-about-going-short-term-mission-trips. For typical stages experienced during cultural transition, see ism.intervarsity.org/resource/your -cross-cultural-journey.

[3]Lewis Hyde, *The Gift: Creativity and the Artist in the Modern World* (New York: Vintage, 2007), 43.

[4]Ibid., 11.

[5]Ibid., 46-47.

[6]Ibid., 26.

[7]Ronald Rolheiser, *Sacred Fire: A Vision for a Deeper Human and Christian Maturity* (New York: Image, 2014).

[8]"Ignatian Spirituality," accessed April 30, 2016, www.bc.edu/bc_org/prs /stign/ignatian_spirit.html.

[9]Rolheiser, *Sacred Fire*, 249.

[10]Ibid., ix.

7 TRANSLATING CHANGE

[1]Francis Chan, "How Not to Make Disciples," www.vergenetwork .org/2011/10/19/francis-chan-how-not-to-make-disciples-video/.

[2]Ibid.

[3]G. K. Chesterton, *Heretics* (Nashville: Sam Torode Book Arts, 2011), 78.

[4]Ibid., 80.

[5]See "Experiential Learning Experience (ELI)," Messiah College, www .messiah.edu/info/21610/experiential_learning_initiative.

[6]Scott Willyerd, "Why a College is Using PR Terminology for Student Success," *Huffington Post*, updated July 29, 2015, www.huffingtonpost .com/scott-willyerd/why-a-college-is-using-pr_b_7889676.html.

[7]Paolo Freire, *Pedagogy of the Oppressed* (New York: Herter and Herter, 1970), 60.

[8]Email with Jennifer Dukes Lee, April 21, 2016.

[9]In 2008, doctoral candidate James T. Neill presented findings from a longitudinal study on "the impacts of outdoor education programs." The study involved several thousand participants and looked at changes in eleven "life effectiveness" skills. Results showed "moderately positive short-term changes [in 3,640 participants], and small-moderate long-term changes [in 663]. . . . The largest changes were evident for emotional control, self confidence, social competence, task leadership, and time management." "Enhancing Life Effectiveness: The Impact of Outdoor Education Programs," University of Western Sydney, May 2009, wilderdom.com/phd2/Neill2008EnhancingLifeEffectivenessTheImpacts OfOutdoorEducationPrograms.pdf.

What was absent in Neill's study, but what is present in many outdoor programs like XD, are the moral and spiritual components. I don't expect a weeklong backpacking trip to change a participant's time management, though it happens, as it did with Rob. I am more optimistic about experience-inspired insights happening (for example, "I recognize now that my selfishness hurts others and that Jesus desires relational healing"), which often lead to changes in day-to-day living.

[10]T. S. Eliot, *Four Quartets* (New York: Harcourt, 1943).

[11]Makenna D. Huff, "A Walk Down Memory Lane: How Ritualized Movement Creates Sacred Space on the Camino de Santiago" (religion major capstone thesis, Ohio Wesleyan University, April 24, 2015), 3.

[12]For preparing and processing a mission trip, see InterVarsity's Global Programs Journal at store.intervarsity.org/global-projects-journal -guide-each.html.

[13]Ann Kroeker, "Seeing the World," March 23, 2011, www.theologyofwork .org/the-high-calling/blog/seeing-world www.thehighcalling.org/articles /essay/seeing-world.

[14]*Lost Boys of Sudan*, POV, 2003, www.lostboysfilm.com/index.html.

8 NAVIGATING VALLEYS

[1]Ronald Rolheiser, *Sacred Fire: A Vision for a Deeper Human and Christian Maturity* (New York: Image, 2014), 250.

[2]Ibid.

[3]Ibid., 251.

[4]Simone Weil, *Waiting for God* (New York: Perennial Classics, 2001), xxxi.

[5]Kenneth R. Kalisch, *The Role of the Instructor in the Outward Bound Educational Process* (Kearney, NE: Morris Publishing, 1999), 7.

[6]William G. Syrotuck, *Analysis of Lost Person Behavior* (Mechanicsburg, PA: Barkleigh Productions, 2000), 19.

[7]Helen Cepero, *Christ-Shaped Character: Choosing Love, Faith and Hope* (Downers Grove, IL: InterVarsity Press, 2014), 75.

[8]Ibid., 76.

[9]Rolheiser, *Sacred Fire*, 251.

[10]Henri Nouwen, "Bringing Solitude into Our Lives," *Devotional Classics: Selected Readings for Individuals and Groups*, ed. Richard J. Foster and James Bryan Smith (San Francisco: HarperSanFrancisco, 1993), 97.

9 GETTING UNSTUCK TOGETHER

[1]Automated Morningness-Eveningness Questionnaire, Center for Environmental Therapeutics, www.cet-surveys.com/index.php?sid=61524&newtest=Y.

[2]Richard M. Gula, SS, *The Good Life: Where Morality and Spirituality Converge* (New York: Paulist Press, 1999), 16.

[3]For a conversation about this, go to Fan Theories, "The reason why Edna says 'no cape' and why she gave Syndrome one," www.reddit.com/r/FanTheories/comments/3eshvu/the_incredibles_the_reason_why_edna_says_no_capes/.

[4]Richard M. Gula, SS, *Reason Informed by Faith: Foundations of Catholic Ministry* (New York: Paulist Press, 1989), 65.

[5]*The Barkley Marathons: The Race That Eats Its Young*, 2016, barkleymovie.com/.

[6]Brian Dalen, "The 2016 Barkley Marathons: One Person Finishes!," *Runner's World*, April 5, 2016, www.runnersworld.com/races/the-2016-barkley-marathons-one-person-finishes.

[7]Ibid.

[8]"Pulse Is Hiring!," *Pulse*, www.pulsepittsburgh.org.

[9]"Effects of Hurricane Mitch in Honduras," Wikipedia, en.wikipedia.org/wiki/Effects_of_Hurricane_Mitch_in_Honduras.

[10]Email with Jennifer Dukes Lee, April 21, 2016.

[11]Helen Cepero, *Christ-Shaped Character: Choosing Love, Faith and Hope* (Downers Grove, IL: InterVarsity Press, 2014), 145.

[12]Ibid.

[13]"Leadership and Discipleship in the Wilderness," ccojubilee.org/stu dents/events-trips/leadership-and-discipleship-in-the-wilderness -ldw/30/.

[14]"Ocean City Beach Project," ccojubilee.org/students/events-trips/ocean -city-beach-project/33/.

[15]Gula, *Reason Informed by Faith*, 65.

EPILOGUE

[1]C. H. Dodd, *The Bible Today* (Cambridge, England: University Press, 1965), 51-52.

[2]"Amanda Doom Helps Rescue Trafficked Children," CCO, ccojubilee.org /stories/amanda-doom-helps-rescue-trafficked-children/83/.

SMALL GROUP STUDY GUIDE

[1]For an in-depth guide to listening, see Sherod Miller and Phyllis A. Miller, *Core Communication: Skills and Process* (Evergreen, CO: Interpersonal Communication Programs, 1997).

[2]Paul Angone, "25 Signs You Are Having a Quarter Life Crisis," allgroanup .com/adult/25-signs-quarter-life-crisis/.

APPENDIX A

[1]Ronald Rolheiser, *Sacred Fire: A Vision for a Deeper Human and Christian Maturity* (New York: Image, 2014), 103.

[2]Ibid., 104.

ABOUT THE AUTHOR

Sam Van Eman is a resource specialist for CCO's Experiential Designs team, where he cocreates transformational experiences for college students, professionals, and organizations. As a public speaker and facilitator, he has taught (and played) in barns and boardrooms, canyons, classrooms, and auditoriums. His years on campus resulted in numerous Christian Service awards for his student leaders and a Greek Life brotherhood award named in his honor.

He has contributed to *PRISM Magazine*, the Center for Parent/Youth Understanding, *Christianity Today*'s Faith in the Workplace, and was highlighted in the decade's best at *Catapult Magazine*. He is the author of *On Earth as It Is in Advertising? Moving from Commercial Hype to Gospel Hope* and lives with his wife and two daughters in central Pennsylvania.

ABOUT THE CCO

The Coalition for Christian Outreach (CCO) calls college students to serve Jesus with their entire lives. The CCO is distinct in three ways:

1. We develop students to be passionate leaders who serve Jesus Christ in their studies, jobs, communities, and families.

2. We serve together with the church, inviting students into the lives of local congregations.

3. We design each ministry to fit the needs of every campus we serve.

Learn more at ccojubilee.org.

ABOUT XD

Experiential Designs (XD) is a department of the CCO that offers creative opportunities for transformation. Over its forty-year history, XD has grown into a community of experiential trainers, leadership educators, outdoor professionals, and program developers who collaborate to deliver customized learning moments. Our approach connects desired outcomes to a robust understanding of being human, while leaving space for God to move in and through our designs. Our services range from local leadership and professional development programs to global adventure, service, and travel expeditions.

For full descriptions of all of our services, see our online catalog. Learn more at ccojubilee.org/about-cco-xd.